"Draves knows how the Internet is changing the education experience."
Judy Bryan, Culture Editor, Wired News, Wired.com

"A must read for administrators, teachers and anyone interested in the power and the future of online learning and teaching."
Jan Wahl, San Diego State University, San Diego, CA

"Draves has approached this timely topic in a functional, no-nonsense way. His book is pleasantly void of jargon and annoying filler — he gets down to the issue at hand and approaches it in a refreshing manner."
Greg Johnson, El Segundo, CA

"Draves' hands-on sensibility is useful for those of us that believe we need to stay up on the leading edge of learning. Read this book."
Julia King Tamang, University of Oregon, Portland, OR

"What educators need to know now — whether they are exploring possibilities of teaching online, or are already actively engaged in this important medium. A great book!"
Rita Martinez-Purson, Santa Fe Community College, Santa Fe, NM

"Draves is the most savvy, non-techie Internet guru I have ever known."
Cem Erdem, ADC Telecommunications, a billion-dollar Internet company

"This book showed me just what to do to make my own online course enjoyable to teach and successful in the marketplace."
Ron Gross, author of Peak Learning

D1133907

Advanced Teaching Online
Third Edition

William A. Draves

Published by LERN Books, a division of the Learning Resources Network (LERN), P.O. Box 9, River Falls, Wisconsin 54022, U.S.A.

Library of Congress Cataloging In Publication Data
Draves, William A., 1949-
    Teaching Online, second edition

ISBN 1-57722-027-7

Printing
7   6   5   4   3   2   1

Dedication

Several years ago I discovered that my oldest son, Jason, was more computer literate than I would ever be. I began asking him questions, and then asking his friends questions. I looked over his shoulder at his chat room, watched him develop a part-time business on the Web, and saw him do his homework using the resources of the Web. Jason has been on the cutting edge of life in the Information Age, and I have learned much from him.

When Sammie Jackson came to live with us, I was bent on mentoring him through high school. In a few short months it became apparent that I would learn more from him than I could teach him. Sammie understood another culture, another way of thinking, another value system. He also believed that race and culture should make no difference; he judged no one by their color, and he asked the same in return. Sammie has been on the cutting edge of culture in the Information Age, and I have learned much from him.

When Willie was just two years old, I took him, his crayons and paper with me while shopping. The store keeper looked at Willie's drawing and told him he would be an artist some day. Willie looked up and firmly replied, "I am an artist." A child of the 21st century, Willie can envision space travel while I cannot. He can think about life a million years ago, or hence. He can also draw, make up jokes, and write a great fictional story. Willie is on the cutting edge of art and relationships in the Information Age, and I have learned much from him.

I dedicate this book to my three sons, Jason Coates, Sammie Jackson, and Willie Draves, representatives of the online generation who have taught me much about the 21st century.

Cover Artwork

The artwork on the cover of the book is done by Gina Capaldi of San Dimas, California. It first appeared on the brochure cover of the Los Angeles Harbor College Extension Program in Wilmington, Calif., Carla Mussa-Muldoon, director. Both the artist and the continuing education program have a knack for hitting on important themes in our culture. For this author, the drawing of the Scarecrow on the Internet connected the transition of the last century, as represented by the L.Frank Baum book *The Wizard of Oz,* with the current transition to the Information Age and learning online.

Acknowledgments

For this third edition of *Advanced Teaching Online*, I am indebted to the online pioneers with whom I have worked.

They include online learning authorities Dr. Rita-Marie Conrad, Rena Palloff, Keith Pratt, and Les Howles. The more than 6,000 faculty who have taken our online courses have contributed much, and some fifty of their best ideas are included in the book.

The LERN staff, leaders and consultants continue to be supportive and the best team for which someone could ever hope. Chairs of the Board during this writing include: Mr. Kim Roberts, Perth, Australia; Pete Hangen, Virginia Beach, VA; Cecilia Bowie, Chicago; Doug Soo, Vancouver, BC; and Dee Baird, Cedar Rapids, IA.

Production was carried out professionally, as always, by Danita Dickinson.

Table of Contents

Part I.
Learning in the
21st Century

Chapter 1
Lifelong Learning
in the 21ˢᵗ Century

Throughout the 10,000 history of humankind, no one taught on the Internet. Teaching online is a totally new experience. And it is taking place as part of an economic, social and education transformation of the way we work, live and learn in the Information Age of the 21ˢᵗ century.

Teaching online is not the same as teaching in-person. It is not simply being able to use a new technology, like a slide projector or fax machine. The Internet is not just a tool.

What we are seeing is that online learning is transforming education as a whole. Generation Y, the first generation of the 21ˢᵗ century, is more comfortable with technology than any previous generation in history (Coates, 2007, page 119). According to *Generational Learning Styles* by Julie Coates, Gen Y learns well by interacting with their colleagues, leading to innovative and effective collaborative learning techniques.

Student collaboration can also involve more traditional instructor roles, such as using student engagement even in evaluating individual student learning. Engaging students in the evaluation process not only can save faculty time but also enhance the measurement of learning outcomes, according to Rita-Marie Conrad and J. Ana Donaldson, authors of *Engaging the Online Learner* (Conrad and Donaldson, 2004, page 27).

The economic transformation for post-industrial societies is from the industrial age of factories and offices to the information age of knowledge workers and professional services. Where is all this headed? Most likely toward teaching

The Internet also gives us as teachers an unprecedented opportunity

1

to treat learners as individuals, helping them to strengthen their unique strengths and address their individual weaknesses.

It is clear that we all do not learn one way, at one speed, or at one proficiency. In preparing students to be knowledge workers, we are at our best when we can treat each student as an individual. That is one reason why the United Kingdom has set the pedagogical goal of "personalisation (sic) and choice" as a new guiding principle for education in this century, according to leading British educator professor Diana Laurillard (Department of Education and Training, United Kingdom, Laurillard, 2005).

Advanced Teaching Online shows you how to develop and teach your online course. If you are new to online learning, you will find this a comprehensive guidebook to the fundamentals of developing and teaching an online course.

If you are experienced in online learning, you will find advanced techniques and information you won't find anywhere else. There is advanced information about creating audio lectures, continuous engagement in maintaining the online conversation, using statistics to track patterns in student online comments, new assessment techniques, and much more. Then challenge yourself to the Best Practices Checklist and benchmark your teaching.

After reading *Advanced Teaching Online*, you will have the latest and most advanced information about developing and teaching an online course. You will know how the Internet is changing how we learn, how to plan your online course, how to develop content, interaction and assessment, how to teach online, and much more.

Welcome to the 21st century. Welcome to online learning.

The Story of Oz

The Wizard of Oz was written a little over 100 years ago, in 1900. The movie came out in 1939. *The Wizard of Oz* is about the transition society was going through at that time. Up until that time we were an agrarian society. Most people earned their living by farming.

L. Frank Baum saw that things were going to be different, that we were going to move into what would become known as the Industrial Age. He knew that life would be totally different.

Baum understood somehow that the attitudes and the values of the agrarian pastoral society, which people had known, and he had known, and was the height of civilization — all that was going to change. He was against that change. He thought the transition was awful. So he created the scarecrow and the tin man and the lion to represent the virtues of the agrarian society. In his time, Kansas was regarded as a land of prosperity and goodness. That's why Baum set his story in Kansas, because he was indicating that even in beautiful Kansas this awful transition is happening.

Now, 100 years later, we are going through another gut-wrenching total change in society. It's not just a new century to which we are witness. It is the moving from one age, the Industrial Age that all of us adults have grown up in and known, and moving into the next age, which is the Information or Internet Age.

That's why we chose for the cover graphic of this book the scarecrow on the Internet, representing the parallel transitions of yesterday and today.

Chapter 2
How the Internet Is Changing How We Learn

The Internet is the biggest technological change in education and learning since the advent of the printed book some 500 years ago. It is destroying the traditional classroom and replacing it with an even better way to learn and teach. And almost every learning situation will be totally altered, including training for business and industry, customer education, association conferences and meetings, continuing education, Sunday School classes, leisure learning, college degree programs, even elementary and secondary school education.

Learners learn more, while working at their own speed, time and manner, over the Internet. There is more interaction among teachers and learners than traditional in-person presentations; daily quizzes can tell you exactly what you have mastered and what areas you still need to work on. Learners and teachers can come from all over the world, and they are able to form a virtual community that will kindle long-term relationships.

In the 21st century, online learning will constitute 50% of all learning and education. The rapid rise of learning on the Internet is occurring not because it is more convenient, cheaper, or faster, but because cognitive learning on the Internet is better than learning in-person. Of the growing number of experts seeing this development, Gerald Celente, author of the popular book *Trends 2000*, summarizes it most succinctly: "Interactive, on-line learning will revolutionize education. The education revolution will have as profound and as far-reaching an effect upon the world as the invention of printing. Not only will it affect where we learn, it also will influence how we learn and what we learn" (Celente, 1997, page 249).

5

As early as 1994, Starr Roxanne Hiltz wrote, "Results are superior in the Virtual Classroom for well-motivated and well-prepared students who have adequate access to the necessary equipment and who take advantage of the opportunities provided for increased interaction with their professor and with other students, and for active participation in the course."

Recent research reported in the *Washington Post* cites studies showing that online learning is equally as effective as learning in-person. And note that we state "cognitive learning," not all learning.

It is still very early in the development of online learning. But the outlines of the potential of online learning are already emerging. The best guide to the next century lies in history, and in examples of technological transition from the nineteenth to the twentieth century. The automobile and tractor were the driving forces for the Industrial Age. The tractor eventually was demonstrated not only to cover more acres than a horse-drawn plow, but to plow deeper (read: better) and thus increase productivity.

Some sectors of society clung to the horse-drawn vehicle, of course. The military still had a cavalry in 1939 to confront Hitler's tanks before the obvious mismatch was addressed (Davis, 1993). The tractor changed education for the 20th century as well. Prior to the tractor and automobile, one-room schoolhouses were placed every six miles so that a child would have to walk at most three miles to school. The one-room schoolhouse necessitated one teacher and multiple grade levels in one room. With the automobile, people moved into towns, and even rural residents could take buses to school, thus causing school consolidation and the eventual all-but-extinction of the one-room schoolhouse. In the State of Washington, for example, between 1935 and 1939 almost 20% of rural one-room schoolhouses were closed.

And when online learning is combined with a more interactive and facilitative in-person learning, it will easily out perform today's outmoded one-size-fits-all traditional lecture delivery system. "Digital media and Internet communications will transform learning practices," notes Peter J. Denning of George Mason University in his *How We Will Learn* (1996, page 2).

Perhaps the most dramatic change is how the Internet is changing how we learn. Distance has nothing to do with "distance education." By this I mean that even when the teacher is in close proximity to the learners, the quality of the cognitive learning and teaching will be higher when the cognitive part of the learning is conducted over the Internet. Keoko University in Japan, for example, is already establishing online learning for its on-campus students (Eisenstodt, 1997).

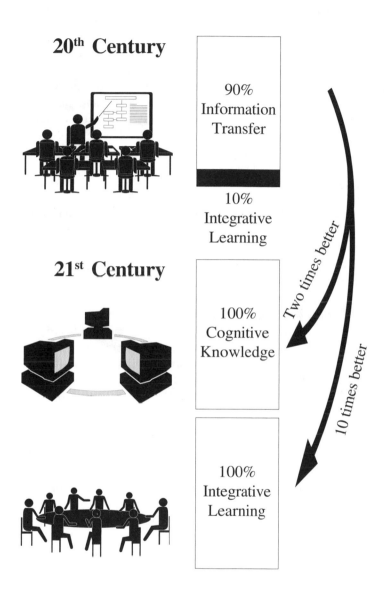

20th Century

90%
Information
Transfer

10%
Integrative
Learning

21st Century

100%
Cognitive
Knowledge

100%
Integrative
Learning

Two times better

10 times better

The Internet is breaking apart the traditional lecture or presentation style of teaching and learning. Two new formats are emerging: online learning, and a different in-person style of learning and teaching.

In this chapter I will outline what we already know and can forecast about how the Internet and online learning are changing how we learn. We know, for example, that the economic force driving life in the 21st century is the microchip and the Internet, just as the automobile was the economic force for change in the 20th century. And we know that business will need workers to learn more, more quickly, and at a lower cost, to remain competitive. We will show that these market forces will create the need and desirability for online learning.

Information Transfer

For most of history the standard educational setting has been an instructor (or teacher, leader, presenter, or speaker) standing in front of a group of people. This is the most common learning design in society, whether it be for college credit classes, noncredit courses, training in business and industry, high school instruction, or even a Sunday School class.

More Feedback, More Consistently

My experience in taking online classes and in teaching them convinces me that students actually get more feedback, more consistently, in a forum such as this (online) class. I think there is a sense of anticipation on the part of the student to return to the online setting to see the responses to his or her questions.
— Mariana Russell

Basically, 90% of all education has been "information transfer," the process of transferring information and knowledge from the teacher's head into the heads of the learners. To do that, teachers have had to talk most of the time. And right up until today that mode of delivery has been the most effective, most efficient, most desirable way to learn.

But as educators we know that the traditional lecture is not the only way to learn. We as learners learn in many different ways, at different times, and from a variety of sources. We also know that learning is not purely a cognitive process, but that it also involves the emotions and even the spirit.

The Internet is destroying the traditional educational delivery system of an instructor speaking, lecturing, or teaching in front of one or more learners.

The whole discipline of self-directed learning, variously called adult learning or adult education, has shown that the traditional delivery system is only one way to learn. The Internet represents the biggest technological aid helping people to learn in 500 years, according to many educators (Thieme, 1996).

What the Internet is doing is exploding the traditional method of teaching into two parts — cognitive learning, which can be accomplished better with online learning; and affective learning, which can be accomplished better in a small group discussion setting.

Why Cognitive Learning Can Be Done Better on the Internet

Cognitive learning includes facts, data, knowledge, mental skills — what you can test. And information transfer and cognitive learning — even critical thinking skills — can be achieved faster, cheaper and better online.

There are several ways that online learning can be better than classroom learning, such as:

- A learner can learn during her or his peak learning time. My peak learning time is from 10 am to noon. My stepson's peak learning time is between midnight and 3 am. He recently signed up for an Internet course and is looking for a couple more, because as he put it, "I have a lot of free time between midnight and 3 am." With traditional in-person classes, only some learners will be involved during their peak learning time. The rest will not fully benefit.

- A learner can learn at her or his own speed. With traditional classes, a learner has one chance to hear a concept, technique or piece of knowledge. With online learning, a learner can replay a portion of audio, reread a unit, review a video, and retest him or herself.

- A learner can focus on specific content areas. With traditional classes, each content area is covered and given the relative amount of emphasis and time that the teacher deems appropriate. But in a ten unit course, a given learner will not need to focus on each unit equally. For each of us, there will be some units we know already and some where we have little knowledge. With online learning, we as learners can focus more time, attention and energy on those units, modules or sections of the course where we need the most help and learning.

- A learner can test himself daily. With online learning, a learner can take quizzes and tests easily, instantly receiving the results and finding out how well she or he is doing in a course.

9

The Internet is like an automobile one hundred years ago. It is still being improved upon.

- A learner can interact more with the teacher. Contrary to common opinion today, online learning is more personal and more interactive than traditional classroom courses. In an online course, the instructor has to create the information transfer part of the course — lectures, graphics, text, video — only once. Once the course units or modules have been developed, there is need only for revisions later on. The instructor is then free to interact with participants in the course.

Learners can acquire the data and facts faster using the Internet. Officials at University Online Publishing, which has been involved in online learning more than most organizations, say that a typical 16-week college course, for example, can be cut to 8 weeks because students learn more quickly online.

Finally, technology has consistently driven down costs. Recent reports indicate that education costs are grew at over 5% for 1998, well above the 3% average for all other sectors of the economy. With education costs in the traditional system soaring, technological innovations promise the ability to deliver an education more cheaply.

Downward pressure is already being exerted on prices by online courses. Officials at Regents College in Albany, NY, which collects data on 8,000 distance learning courses, say that prices are dropping already. One community college in Arizona, for example, offers online courses at just $32/credit hour for in-state residents, and $67/credit hour for out-of-state learners.

More Interaction Occurs with Online Learning

The heart and soul of an online course is not the lecture, the delivery, the audio, or video. Rather, it is the interaction between the participants and the teacher, as well as the interaction among the participants themselves. This daily interaction among participants, for example, helps form what John Hagel, author of *Net Gain* (1997), calls a "virtual community," and what some educators call a "learning community."

The next time you are in a class, count the number of questions asked of the teacher during a one-hour time period. Because of the instructor's need to convey information, the time able to be devoted to questions is very short. In an online course, everyone can ask questions, as many questions as each learner wants or needs.

There is more discussion. In an online course, there is more discussion. If there is a group discussion with thirty people and six to eight people make comments, that is a successful discussion that will take up almost a whole hour. Almost everyone in the group will agree it was lively. Now if you go into an asynchronous discussion forum on the Internet, and thirty people are there, and six to eight are making comments, you will conclude that the discussion is lagging.

The same number of comments on the Internet do not appear to be as lively a discussion as when delivered in person because the capability and capacity of the Internet is that every person can make comments—at the same time. A transcript of a typical online discussion would take hours to give verbally. Online, we can participate in discussions easily, absorbing more information in a much shorter time and engaging in more interaction, not less.

Top Ten Reasons

To review, here are my top ten reasons why cognitive learning on the Internet is BETTER than traditional in-person presentations:

Number 10. You can learn at your own peak learning time of day.

Number 9. You can learn at your own speed.

Number 8. You can learn faster.

Number 7. You can interact more with the teacher and other participants.

Number 6. There are more topics and subjects online.

Number 5. Participants come from around the world.

Number 4. You can learn from the foremost authorities and experts.

Number 3. Online learning is less expensive and thus more accessible.

Number 2. Internet links provide more resources.

Number 1. You can form a virtual community.

The Forces Driving Online Learning

Online learning is popular and becoming more popular all the time. At the time of this writing, it is estimated that close to two million people are learning online. Many college students, including adult students, like online learning because it allows greater flexibility in the scheduling of their time. In 2000, the first high school, in Toronto, was reported to be requiring its students to take online courses. In the same year, the first university, Farleigh Dickinson, was reported to be instituting a requirement that students take at least one online course a year.

This is just the beginning. There are several forces that are turning this scenario for online learning into reality, and turn it into reality very quickly. They include:

Business. Business is the biggest force. Business now understands that in order to remain competitive and profitable, it will need employees who are learning constantly. The only cost effective way for this to happen is with online learning.

So business will require its people to learn online, and it will look to recruit college graduates who can learn online. Colleges and universities will quickly adopt online learning because business will demand that capability from their graduates.

Drop Rates

The interactivity is what distinguishes between a class and a correspondence course. We have both at my school. The interactive courses have drop rates similar to F2F classes, while the e-mail correspondence courses tend to run 60-85% drops. — Mike Felker, South Plains College, Levelland, TX

Youth. Young people want to learn online. They understand the future, because it is the world in which they must work and compete. Young students will choose online learning.

Marketplace. There area enormous opportunities created by online learning. There are subjects previously unavailable face-to-face that can now be offered successfully online. There are people in various localities that have not previously been served who can now take online courses. Competitors and other educational providers looking for new niches and markets are another force driving online learning.

The Impact of Online Learning

Online learning is rapidly becoming recognized as a valid learning delivery system. The number of part-time students in higher education, to name just one educational system, now outnumbers full-time students. The number of colleges offering online courses has soared. Online graduate programs and certificate programs have doubled over one year ago. Online learning has grown exponentially in the business sector, according to Elliot Masie of Saratoga Springs, NY, one of the foremost experts on online training in the workforce. Surveys by the American Society for Training and Development (ASTD) see online training replacing much of on-site training in the near future.

Online learning will do for society what the tractor did for food. A century ago food was expensive, in limited supply, and with very little variety. Today food is relatively cheap, in great supply in our society, and with tremendous variety. The Internet will do the same for education. More people will be able to learn more, for much less cost, and with a tremendous variety in choice of topics and subjects. It is something that societies of the past could only dream about. And it will come true for us in a very short time.

Chapter 3
Learning in Person

This book is about teaching online. But in order to understand the full context in which online learning will occur, it is good to know something about how people will learn in-person in the 21st century.

As we have noted, about half of all learning will occur online. That leaves the other half to be done in-person, but only a small portion of in-person will be the traditional lecture format we have today and that characterized almost all learning in the 20th century. Traditional lecture teaching will decline because information transfer can be done more effectively online. Most learning in-person will be very different from in-person learning today. In person, or face-to-face (F2F), learning will be focused around what the Internet cannot do. It will be oriented around the integrational aspects of learning. It will be learner-centered.

Some learning, maybe 20%, can be done totally online. If you want to know about how to put a computer together, or maybe the history of the Civil War in the United States, you are interested in facts and data. You don't need a group discussion.

And some learning, maybe 20%, will be done entirely in-person. For example, if you want to learn how to make more ethical decisions as a business manager, you don't need a lot of facts and data. Instead, you will benefit from working with a teacher and perhaps other business managers dealing with the same issue.

And there will be a large portion of learning, maybe 60%, that will best be delivered using both online learning formats combined with integrative in-person discussion learning. Using both online and in-person formats, learners will gain the cognitive knowledge and facts from teachers online, and then meet with a facilitator/teacher in-person to enhance and integrate their learning.

For example, a poetry writing class might involve an online module from a prize winning poet, combined with an in-person class with a local poetry instructor who can review the participants' work and make more personal and individual suggestions on writing poetry.

We actually know a lot less about how people learn in-person than we do about how people learn online. That is because online learning is almost entirely cognitive, and we have studied and practiced cognitive learning — transferring facts, information, data and knowledge--for thousands of years.

Posting course material

Perhaps oddly enough, my first-time use of Internet web pages to post course material came when the department's copier was highly restricted and each copy was charged. I knew that students had free access to printing at computer stations across campus, so my syllabus cost virtually nothing! Once I had this material on-line, I found that there were many helpful sites for students to use and I posted these in addition to the syllabus. — Carol Ann Stevens, Buffalo State University, Buffalo, NY

Integrative learning, the kind that best takes place in-person, has been practiced much less because teachers have had to spend almost all of their time on information transfer, leaving precious little time for discussions, affective learning, unlearning, and other forms of integrative learning.

We can forecast that most in-person learning will take place with the participants and teacher sitting in chairs in a circle. This is the room arrangement most conducive to discussion and interaction.

And we know what we want in-person classes and meetings to accomplish. Here are some of the things that we will want in-person classes and meetings to accomplish:
- Help the participants learn how to learn.
- Encourage each learner, provide positive feedback and motivation.
- Deal with the emotions of learning.
- Help each person integrate the cognitive knowledge gained into his or her own life, the learner's own context, relevancy, and meaning.
- Address the spiritual aspects of learning.

Projected Learning

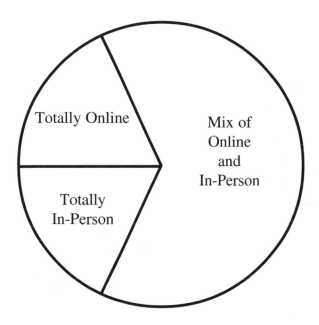

How much learning will be online during the course of the 21ˢᵗ century.

- Help learners unlearn old ideas; assist them in "grieving for their old ideas," as adult educator Jerold Apps puts it.
- Measure the integrative learning needs of the learner.
- Assess the integrative learning outcomes.
- Advise learners on their own learning directions, their best learning styles.
- Create dissonance, challenging concepts and helping to stretch individuals' minds and frames of reference.
- Help learners ask the right questions.
- Relate learning to action, assisting participants to incorporate their newfound learning into a change in behavior, either individual behavior or social change actions.
- Physically transmit a bonding between learner and other learners, or between learner and teacher, to facilitate and heighten awareness and that "teachable moment."
- Create new learning as a group that could not be accomplished individually.

"Just for Fun" Section Helps Discussion

I have a section on my discussion board entitled *Just for Fun* that has links to wacky sites I find each week. It breaks up the class and provides a way to start a discussion. For example, this week's listing was a quiz: "What kind of dog breed are you?" They were guessing mine. It provided a rather lively discussion. — Candyce Duggan, Southwestern College, Wichita, KS

I am using the term "integrative learning" to encompass all of the above. Integrative learning implies incorporating one's learning into a greater system of understanding, making sense of the knowledge, being able to master it — not simply repeat it — internalize it, and use it.

The kind of teacher required for in-person learning will need to have very different skills and abilities from the kind of skills most teachers possess today. A cliché has already been created to summarize the transition: "The sage on the stage will be replaced by the guide on the side."

In-person teachers will need to know how to lead a good discussion, how to create dissonance and dialogue, how to summarize and bring things together, how to deal with the emotions of learning, how to advise learners, and most importantly, be more focused on the learners than on the subject matter. The in-person teacher will be a moderator, facilitator, advisor, counselor, broker, mentor.

The adult educator Jerry Apps has been an early pioneer in exploring this kind of learning. Here's what he says, "I emphasize an approach to teaching adults where you, the teacher, engage your entire personality, how you think, what you know and how you know it, and how you feel and why you feel that way. As a teacher, you ought to be prepared to help learners understand the meaning of what they are learning, help them explore and create, and help them critically analyze as well as think introspectively."

Students' Online Comments.
I find a couple of interesting phenomena: 1) students are very kind and supportive online; 2) students take more risks with their comments and observations online and are more inclined to illustrate their views with personal anecdotes or observations; 3) when somebody is struggling, the online group tends to come together to help; 4) when students have the opportunity to think before they speak (type), their comments are more clear and coherent. That makes them feel better about themselves. — Dr. L.J. Tessier, Youngstown State University, Youngstown, OH

The best role model for the in-person teacher I can think of is the elementary school teacher. When my son was in grade school, each one of his teachers could sit down with his mother and me and spend a half-hour talking about my son and his learning.

There is an old saying that "Elementary school teachers love their students; high school teachers love their subject matter; and college professors love themselves." That's probably not fair, but it does illustrate the strengths that elementary school teachers bring to their teaching. They do not pretend to be subject experts. Instead, they are focused on helping their students learn, and their greatest expertise is understanding the learners themselves.

You may teach a course online and not have an in-person component to the class or training. You may teach part of your course online, and then also meet with your participants in-person and help facilitate their learning in-person as well. Or you may market your online course to other teachers and trainers who will conduct the in-person aspect of the course or learning. All of these arrangements are being utilized.

In their excellent book, *The Faculty Guide for Moving Teaching and Learning to the Web*, Boettcher and Conrad call traditional face-to-face classes that make some use of the Internet as "web-enhanced courses."

Here are some of the ways you can use the web to enhance your face-to-face class:

1. Post homework assignments on the web.
2. Post quiz or test answers on the web.
3. Post the course outline, bibliography, and syllabus online.
4. Have students submit essays and papers as e-mail attachments.
5. Post student work, such as a paper, on the web.
6. Provide links to useful and relevant web sites.
7. Post relevant articles online.
8. Produce recorded audio of some of your lectures and post it.
9. Hold online discussions in between your face-to-face meetings.
10. Establish student study groups online to assist them in studying for your final exam.
11. Post quizzes or preparatory tests online to help students study for a final test.

Just about anything that can be done in an online course can also be done as a supplement or aid in the conducting of a face-to-face course as well. If you are teaching a face-to-face class and interested in using the web to enhance your course, the rest of this book will provide more detail on each of the above web strategies.

In this book we will assume you are teaching a stand-alone online course without an in-person component to it. But it is useful to understand how in-person learning can complement and enhance the online learning.

Part II.
Planning Your
Online Course

Chapter 4
The Technology
of Online Learning

In order to teach successfully online, you do need to know how the technology works and how the Internet works.

However, you don't have to become a techie. Some online classroom software allow you to teach online with very little technical knowledge. Or you may decide to learn how to work with the technology. Or you may decide to have someone else with technology skills do the technical aspects for you.

In this section we deal with the information about technology that all online teachers should know.

History of the Internet

The Internet was created in the 1970s by a collaboration between the United States government and researchers and scientists in higher education. It started out as a military defense project and quickly broadened to the scientific community, then throughout the rest of the university, then to the private sector and the public. The Internet is a physical connection of millions of computers. So the Internet is millions of computers linked to each other, initially via phone lines. As the Internet grew in popularity, the government released various maintenance functions to the private sector to allow for the Internet's continued growth and usefulness.

The World Wide Web was created in 1991 by Tim Berners-Lee, who worked at a nonprofit scientific and research agency in Switzerland known by its acronym CERN. The Internet linked all the computers together, but there was not a common language recognized by all the computers, and there wasn't a standard way to locate information on any given computer (server).

Berners-Lee invented the Uniform Resource Locator (URL), or the address system we use today, which begins http://, often followed by www.

He created HTML, or hypertext marking language, so that files and information could be put into a common language so all computers could read the information.

And he invented the hyperlinking system, where you and I can click on an underlined item and jump to another file on another computer.

Shortly thereafter an undergraduate student at the University of Illinois in Champaign-Urbana invented the first browser, software that allows us to search the world wide web for web sites and information.

Thus, the creation of the Internet and the World Wide Web was largely the result of work of those in the nonprofit and education sector. At the core, the creation of the Internet and World Wide Web has less to do with commercial or business enterprise and more to do with information and services that impact the general public and the majority of citizens. Those in the nonprofit and education sectors are still in the forefront of Internet invention. An important and central aspect of the Internet and online culture is online learning and the development of online courses.

How the Technology Works

Specific information, including words, pictures, audio, and video, resides on a particular computer, called a server. You find that information on the server, and pull it over the Internet to your computer. Your computer is often called a "client server."

Some terms and concepts helpful to know include:

IP addresses. Every computer has an address, called an IP number. It is a series of numbers. Your computer has an IP number.

Domain name. This is the address for a particular web site. Since words are easier to remember than a series of numbers, a commission assigns words a specific IP address. So when you type in www.whatever, you go to the IP address assigned to 'whatever.'

Server. This is a computer with files, information, or web sites on it. Most servers are powerful computers minus the keyboard and monitor. They are commonly stored on shelves at an Internet Service Provider (ISP), and continually connected to the Internet. Places with large numbers (hundreds or thousands) of servers are some-times called server farms.

Client server. This is your computer, or any computer accessing the Internet.

Student Tutorial

To help students with the technology of the online course, we created a student tutorial for Blackboard. We are requiring that students complete the Student Tutorial as their first assignment. We even give points to them for doing this. Of course we can't tell if they have read through all the material, but in order to get the points they have to complete two discussions and one five-item quiz.

As a follow up to the above assignment, I then have them post a home page, an introduction in the actual course site they are taking, and download and then submit a contract form that says they have completed the tutorial, read the syllabus, and understood the requirements for the course. The primary purpose of this latter assignment is for them to know how to save a document and then submit a document electronically. The home page and introduction are used to begin this creation of community.

One other thing I do prior to the semester starting is to send out an e-mail (and sometimes a letter) that provides the initial instructions on how to log into the course.

I am finding that the first week is devoted to getting the students into the technology. — Amy Finch, Ft. Hays State University, Hays, KS

Cookies. Cookies are identification tags which tell the server where you are, so it knows where to send the information you want. In order to participate in chats, forums, purchase online or engage in other interactivity, you have to tell the server where you are. Cookies do this.

You should know that when you make a comment in an online chat, you provide your IP address to the host server. So even though you may not sign your real name to a comment, for example, if the people managing the host server wanted to track down a particular comment to a particular IP address, they could. Thus, your "anonymous" comment is far from anonymous.

Tube or Bandwidth. Only so much information can go over a phone line. So there are big phone lines, starting with T1 and going up. And there are cable lines used for television transmission. Simple data, like words, take up less space or bandwidth. Sounds and pictures are much more complicated and take up lots of bandwidth. And when everyone is using the same phone line, there is congestion or heavy traffic.

Plug-ins. Plug-ins are software needed to run a particular program, like RealPlayer to get audio, or MP3 to get music, or Adobe to see graphics. You download the plug-in to your computer.

Basically, your online course will reside on a server, usually your institution's server, although it can be on any server with good connections to the Internet. You will use an online classroom software, which also will reside on that server. You will post content in your online classroom. You and your students will access your online course on the Internet by going to a specific address or URL on the Internet and entering a user name and password to gain access.

This book centers on the educational aspects rather than technical aspects of teaching online. In reviewing a number of books about the technology of online learning, if you want to know more about the technical aspects, I would recommend *How the Internet Works* by Preston Gralla, published by Que, a division of Macmillan Computer Publishing, Indianapolis, IN. A few of the topics covered better there include:

- FTP and downloading files
- How Java, JavaScript, and ActiveX work
- How CGI scripting works
- Video on the Internet
- Animation on the web
- How workgroup software works
- How intranets work
- How markup languages work
- How hypertext works, and much more.

Dealing with Technical Problems

The Internet is like a Model T horse-less carriage around 1905. It breaks down. It isn't perfect. It is a work in progress that will become more consistent, fast, and reliable over time. But like the users of the first cars, first airplanes, first radios, first telephones, and first television sets, you will experience technical problems your grandchildren will not.

A technical problem could occur at any one of the various components of the Internet. They include:

A. Your computer. Some 80% of technical problems are "user problems." That's you. Here's a tip to solve more than half of all your technical problems: reboot. Simply shut your computer down properly, and restart it. Another common problem for online users is that many people have not successfully downloaded a plug-in or software. Test any new plug-in or software to make sure it works before you attempt to engage in your online course.

B. Your organization's network. If you are part of an institution or company, your organization will probably have your computer connected to their network. Your organization decides what can and cannot be done on the network.

C. Your connection to the Internet. You gain access to the Internet by connecting to an Internet Service Provider, or ISP. That connection might experience traffic congestion, it could be affected by a storm, it could undergo some kind of maintenance, upgrade, or reconfiguration.

D. The Internet backbone. From your ISP, you go out onto the main lines of the Internet, called the Internet backbone. Traffic congestion on the Internet is a common problem. Things may load slowly. Audio or video may be garbled or incomplete. Or it may be frequently interrupted. The solution is simply to try later. Maybe fewer people will be using it. Maybe something will have been fixed. Maybe the gods will be with you next time.

E. Server. This is the computer where you are trying to gain access and retrieve information.

The most common problem is that a large number of people try to access the same information at the same time. This slows things down, or sometimes even shuts things down for a short while. Occasionally a server will go down completely and have to be restarted.

Servers go down, but not frequently, not regularly. Yet 'the server must be down' is often one of the first reactions when there is a technical problem. Here's how to tell if the server is down. If even one person, anyone, can access the information (web site, server), then there is nothing wrong with the server or web site. If no one can access the web site, then it could be down.

One student taking one of my online courses repeatedly reported online, "We're not getting the audio here in Nebraska." The web site or server doesn't discriminate geographically. If the web site and server are up, then the problem is elsewhere (connections, client server, your ISP, etc.). If the web site/server is down, then no one can access it.

Hidden Stress

I think that the greatest stress added to everyone is the hidden element of technology. Almost all workers today know that they need to embrace technology in order to keep up in the workplace. However, a self assessment would most likely reveal that a large majority of workers need to do something to increase their technological capabilities. Even those of us that are in the technological field find it very difficult to keep up with the rapid pace of technology, let alone trying to keep up and infuse the technology into our class rooms. — Craig Shaw, Central Community College, Grand Island, NE

Problem Solving

Here are the most commonly used solutions to technical problems:

1. Try it again. Type the command, hit the key, press the button again.
2. Reboot. Shut down your computer and restart it.
3. Wait awhile. Wait an hour. Or less, or more.
4. Check with your ISP. Call your ISP and see if they are experiencing problems.
5. Call your techie. If the none of the first four solutions work, call your techie.

Get a Techie

Everyone needs a techie. Even techies have techies. Regardless of your level of technical ability with your computer, software, and the Internet, you will want a techie for those times when you are unable to solve a technical problem.

Here's how to find your own techie.

First, establish your level of technical capability. You don't have to know anything about your computer except how to turn it on. Don't listen to others who think you have to know how many rams, bytes, bits or mega-k you have. If you want to know how your computer works, fine. If you want to become more technically proficient, good for you. But you don't have to become technically proficient. Establish what you expect you can do technically first, so you know what to ask of your techie.

Second, look to establish a long-term relationship. A long term relationship is one to two years. You need someone who can meet your time requirements (I need you now!) and your budget.

Third, look for someone you trust. I think that's the main requirement. I usually give a techie three tries to fix something. If she or he can't do it after three tries, I am leery of asking that person back.

Also, look for someone whom you trust as a person. Get someone with whom you get along. Get someone you like. Find someone who will be gentle with you, who will make you feel like everything isn't always your fault, and who will teach you a little.

Fourth, look for a student or young person. Most professional techies are very busy and require a good amount of money. You need someone who's available and who will work for very little money. So don't look for someone who makes her or his living from being a techie.

Instead, look for a student or other young person. College or high school students often know a whole lot about computers. They come at a price you can afford. Be generous, pay more than a burger joint, and you will get their loyalty.

Then look to reward your techie in nonmonetary ways. Cookies and love are equally valuable to young techies. If you can provide some compliments, reassurance, and gratitude, this "love" will go a long way in gaining the loyalty of your techie. And perhaps you can do something for your techie, whether it be baking cookies or a job recommendation. The non-monetary rewards are important to all of us in any job.

High school and college students are in every community, almost on every block. You won't have to look far. Take care of your techie, and she or he will take care of you. It's a win-win situation.

When There are Technical Problems

One of my biggest revelations was reading a book about online teaching that stated it is not "if" you have technical problems, but "when" you have technical problems. As an online instructor, you should assume there will be technical problems and create a plan ahead of time for how to deal with your students when a technical problem occurs with your server or course.

One suggestion is to inform students before the course starts what to do if they experience technical problems. Provide a phone number or e-mail address for them to contact. Another suggestion is for you to have all the e-mail addresses of your students so you can quickly e-mail them if there is a problem. And lastly, let them know they won't be missing anything important due to technical failures, that you will extend the time, or repeat the information so as not to create undue pressure on them.

Technology Assessment

For an initial assessment of your students' ability to use technology, have each student create a word document about themselves. The primary purpose is to assess their technical ability. A secondary benefit is the sharing of information about themselves with everyone else in the class. — Jerri Marsee, Union County College, Cranford, NJ

Your Biggest Technical Concern

Your biggest technical concern as an online teacher is simple: losing your data and information. Online teacher and author Ken White advises, "The most important risk-management strategy requires copies of the electronic information on separate storage media. A hard-copy backup is the least technology dependent."

Make a backup copy of everything you write and produce. Keep one or more backup copies on separate computers, disks, zip drives, etc. and think about a paper backup copy as well.

Student Technology Orientation

First time online students commonly experience frustration and problems using technology. A student technology orientation will aid greatly in your student satisfaction, retention, and participation in your online course.

Perhaps your institution has a technology orientation for students, or your online classroom software company has developed one. If not, consider these options:

- Online student tutorial.
- Required activities and mandatory checklist (like testing audio, or posting a document as an attachment).
- A face-to-face student technology orientation.
- Assigning student technology mentors.
- A help line or phone-accessed technical support person.
- Opening your online course one week ahead of time for students to become acquainted with it.
- E-mailing instructions.
- Mailing instructions, sometimes as a duplicate or backup to the e-mailed instructions.

Then be prepared to deal with the technical issues at the start of your course. "I am finding that the first week is devoted to getting the students into the technology," reports experienced online teacher Amy Finch of Fort Hays State University, Hays, Kansas.

—Greg Brecht

Chapter 5
What an Online Classroom Looks Like

Your online course will take place in an online or virtual classroom. It is a password-protected web site where you will post your course content, discuss or dialogue online with your students, create quizzes and measure their learning.

With the area of online learning still very new, some things have not been decided yet. One of those undecided things is what a standard online classroom looks like. So when your students enter your online classroom, they won't immediately be familiar with your online classroom.

Nevertheless, all online classrooms have three common elements:

1. Content
2. Interaction
3. Assessment

Various models of online classrooms are being developed. Eventually a few models will gain greater acceptance and usage than others and become a standard.

As many online classrooms look very much alike, here is what you and your students are likely to find:

You will be given a web site address where you can always find your online classroom. At that web site you will find a request for you to enter your "user name" and "password." Only people registered in your course are given user names and passwords.

When you enter your user name and password, you have "logged on" to the course. There is a record of each student logon, so you can find out how often your students have logged on, and when each student logged on most recently.

Your user name is you. Generally it is your name or some form of your name. Sometimes everyone in the course has the same password. Sometimes you can make up your own password. Often the password appears on the screen as ***** when you type it in so others won't see the password.

After you have successfully entered your user name and password, you have logged on.

Next, you and your students will likely come to a welcome page. Before the course, you will likely create a welcome statement as well as tips and instructions on where your participants should go online and what to do.

From the welcome page, you will see the links or buttons to the other areas of your online classroom.

Following are some common features in each of the three common components: content, interaction, and assessment. Just for reference, people teaching or taking self-study online courses deal with content and assessment. With self-study online courses, sometimes referred to in the training and for-profit sector as eLearning, interaction is very limited or nonexistent. By contrast, interaction is an essential component of teacher-mediated online courses such as you will teach.

Content

The content of online courses is delivered in at least three ways: 1) written and graphic; 2) audio; and 3) video, animation, and moving pictures.

At the time of this writing, many online classrooms are textual in nature, with words and buttons to get from one area to another. Too few are very visual in nature. That will change, as more online classrooms become more visual and graphical.

More and more online courses now have audio lectures with slides. As greater numbers of people have access to the Internet with greater bandwidth, then we will see greater development of video and animation.

Written and Graphic Technology

Written and graphic content is widely available and in use. It is also almost always technically available to anyone who can access the Internet, so you and your other participants should be easily able to use written and graphic technology without any extra hardware or software.

Here is a list of most of the written and graphic capabilities for online learning:

1. <u>Text, lecture notes, instructional presentation</u>. The presenter or instructor can upload her or his lecture notes, text, or instructional presentation and make it available to all participants at any time they want to access it.

   One advantage is that the participant does not need to take notes but can download and print any of the presenter's information. Another key is that the participant can view, or review, the material anytime she or he wants and at the pace, intensity and time commitment that the learner wants.

2. <u>Readings</u>. Related text and lecture notes, readings, references, articles and other information for which distribution permission has been granted can be uploaded and made available to participants.

   Much more information can be made available to participants on a web site than can be found in books. The advantage of readings online, however, is the variety of information, not the length. Reading a lot of information at one time on the web is tedious and a chore. Online information should be chunked, or separated into one to three paragraphs of information at a time.

3. <u>Links to other web sites</u>. Providing links to other web sites and information is a delightful plus in online learning. The links can be in a reference section, but they can also be integrated into the class material and even online discussions or chats.

   For example, many college credit courses establish a relationship with an online library so students in the course can have access to a wealth of other reading materials.

Another illustration is that the instructor or participants can reference a technique, drawing, quote, or explanation on another web site and invite the rest of the participants to click on the address to see the reference immediately.

We have not begun to explore fully the variety and depth of uses that links to other web sites can provide. For example, the participants' list could contain links to the participants' individual home pages with information about each participant, his or her interests, history, and so on that will be a valuable networking and peer learning tool. Such links will give each participant far more information about the other participants than is currently available during in-person introductions.

Someone is constructing our Web Page and I am to keep it updated once it is in place. Thanks again.

From: Marilane Bond (mbond@medadm.emory.edu) Tue Nov 11 13:59:11 EST

Good Afternoon! Marilane Bond from Continuing Medical Education at Emory University in Atlanta, Ga.

From: Sharon Thomas (sharon@hondros.com) Tue Nov 11 14:04:32 EST

As I am someone who learns best by example (particularly, not to repeat bad examples), the Web Pages that Suck site was very helpful! Thanks!

From: Patty Hoerner (phoerner@ccmail.llu.edu) Tue Nov 11 14:11:36 EST

Hello Everyone. I have attended two other presentations given by Lenny Charnoff and have learned immense amounts regarding our web site for continuing dental education. We too are unable to register online at this time. However, I have received our registration form printed out and mailed or faxed to me.

From: lenny charnoff (charnoff@netogether.com) Tue Nov 11 14:13:15 EST

Tnx for the comments on Web Pages That Suck. Go to it :-) Don't worry your web site won't be on it. Another great site is <u>Cool Tool</u> I usually don't recommend sites that are "cool" but this site has a great business model as well as "unorthodox" approaches to life. They also have a collection of web editing tools to look at. It's also a great example of "superb web site"

From: lenny charnoff (charnoff@netogether.com) Tue Nov 11 14:19:46 EST

Brochure On The Web. Great idea. Two caveats. 1. The Web is not print. Be careful that you redesign it for speed, graphics and horizontal format 2. Your brochure on the web should be interactive with plenty of places for your viewer to leave their e-mail address. I have been here since 7:00am pst. One of the great parts about working at home and on the Net is that you get a chance to do things you really like. I'm taking Snulla, my Icelandic mare, for a short ride. Will be back by 1:30pm. Please e-mail me anything and the answer will be in your e-mail tomorrow morning

From: Greg Marshall (computergy@memes.com) Tue Nov 11 14:21:31 EST

Web Tools: Lets not forget Netscape. I use Netscape to create webpages and find it really easier to use and not as proprietary as Frontpage. I also use Office to convert documents, spreadsheets and such into html and then use Netscape to finish the project.

From: Greg Ledford (gledford@mayland.cc.nc.us) Tue Nov 11 14:31:39 EST

Re: Greg Marshall 14:21:31 I agree. My team finds Netscape easier to work with for creating and applying finishing touches. The trick here seems to be Office. Tell me...is this really the best way of importing to html?

This is what a basic discussion forum looks like.

Audio Online Technology

One of the most exciting tools for online learning is audio. Audio is delivered in two ways:
1. Recorded presentations or lectures that can be downloaded to your computer and then played whenever you want.
2. Live, real-time audio like radio.

While some online courses may utilize live, real-time audio, recorded presentations are more common and likely to be found in online courses.

Recorded presentations have tremendous advantages over listening to a teacher live or in-person:
- Students never have to miss a lecture again.
- Participants can listen during their own peak learning times. Students can and should listen to your online lectures during their peak learning time, the time of day when the student is most receptive to learning and able to participate fully.
- Learners can skip ahead. If a student already knows some parts of the online lecture, the student can skip ahead to other parts of the course where the person is either less familiar or wants to pursue more in-depth or advanced material. In this way, students can not just speed up their learning, but their time spent learning will be more interesting, involving, and of value.
- Learners can repeat any part of the online lecture. Some parts of the lecture a particular student may not get the first time or need more time to absorb. You can do that online. And some parts of an online lecture one might enjoy so much someone may want to listen again in order to gain deeper insights or learn something different the second or third time around.

I have one online lecture where there are about 12 minutes that I have played and replayed over a dozen times. Each time I learn something new or reinforce an important point I want to retain.

In order for your students to receive audio, they will need a relatively up-to-date computer (one no older than three years, roughly) with a sound card and speakers. Most computer sold after 2000 have this hardware.

For software, they will need the same plug-in or software as used to record the audio lectures.

There are several wonderful features of recorded online audio, including:
- **Time of presentation.** In the lower right-hand corner, you will see two times. The one to the right is the length of the presentation.

○ Exit ○ New Messages ○ Search ○ Options ○ Logout/in ○ Users ○ Messages

Active threads from last 365 days:

○ New Thread   ○ Refresh

▼ STUDENT COMMENTS

○ June	10/30	(2)
○ Chuck	09/22	(3)
○ Ralph	09/22	(6)
○ Betty	09/16	(3)
○ Susan	08/20	(2)
○ Bill	06/03	(2)
○ August	05/28	(1)
○ Sherri	05/28	(1)
○ May	05/28	(1)
○ April	05/28	(1)
○ Bob	05/28	(1)
○ Chuck T.	05/28	(1)

▲ SUB TOPICS (16)

▲ REFERENCES (5)

○ **Subscribe to Thread**

This is what a threaded bulletin board looks like.

- **Time status.** In the lower right-hand corner, the time on the left tells you how far into the presentation you are right now.
- **Cursor bar.** At the top, you will see a bar that extends as you listen to the audio. You can put your cursor on this bar and move the bar forward or backward. Moving forward, you skip over parts of the presentation you may know already or do not need to hear. Moving backward, you can listen again to any part of the presentation you would like to hear another time.

In addition, your online lectures might also have a written transcript available. Students can use the written transcript of the audio lecture to clarify certain words or phrases, reinforce their listening, or find a particularly useful quote.

To listen to live, real-time audio you use the same software. Unless the lectures are then recorded and posted on the Net afterwards, you are unable to repeat certain parts or get a transcript. And of course you cannot skip ahead.

Whether taped or live, audio provides another enhancement to the learning power of the Internet.

Multimedia and Interaction

Audio presentations are becoming common, and recommended, for online courses. At the time of this writing, other kinds of multimedia, such as video, are optional and used by fewer numbers of online instructors.

The main point with audio, video, animation and simulation is that online courses are moving from text-based courses to multimedia courses, responding to the ways that students learn.

Other kinds of content for online courses include virtual tours, webquests, simulation, games and gaming. At the time of this writing, these kinds of content are positive, optional rather than standard, but growing in usage by online instructors and certainly recommended.

The overall direction here is from more passive to active interaction, with the more interaction and involvement from your students leading to greater learning.

We explore different kinds of content more in Chapter 10.

Animation includes simulations of activities, such as a chemistry experiment. Animations and simulations are becoming more common, and pose wonderful new opportunities for teaching and learning. In one molecular demonstration that this author has seen, students can interact with the simulation, controlling the temperature and the number of

---

Live Chat (IRC)

Carl: Hi, welcome.
Sherry: Thanks, good to be here.
Carl: What's up?
Sherry: Nothing much. How are you?
Carl: I'm great.
Carl: So, what's the biggest issue for you and your organization?
Sherry: Well, that's a big question. Let me start by saying that...

---

molecules, and seeing the resulting interactions, collisions and physical properties. This is a simulation that is not able to be seen or done in a physical laboratory, and thus interactive simulations online are a tremendous learning tool.

Interaction

Interaction takes place in chat rooms, discussion forums, threaded bulletin boards, and/or e-mail. Your online classroom will probably have the following capabilities built in:

E-mail. E-mail capabilities give the instructor and individual participants the opportunity to communicate directly, personally and confidentially. This one-to-one communication allows participants to ask questions, and may lessen the reticence of some participants to venture forward with so-called "stupid" questions, thus encouraging more people to ask more questions.

Asynchronous threaded discussion. One of the truly remarkable and breakthrough technologies provided by the Internet is the opportunity to have an asynchronous group discussion using what is called a "threaded discussion."

The technology allows any participant and the instructors to submit written comments, questions and responses to the chat room, where everyone can read the comments.

"Asynchronous" means that the comments submitted do not have be done at a given time, and that people can read them no matter what time of day they log into the chat.

Live chat rooms. Live chat rooms allow a given number of people to engage in a written group discussion live. The actual number of people allowed varies according to the software program used.

Assessment

The third component of an online course is assessment. Assessment can be done online, or it can be done offline in a face to face situation, depending on your wishes as instructor.

Most online assessment is apt to be a closed-ended question such as multiple-choice format where you click on the answers and hit a submit key. Student answers go to the server's computer, which automatically grades the answers and immediately returns the score and possibly preprogrammed comments for the learner's benefit.

This quiz-test-assessment technology can be used in several ways.

1. Learners can test themselves without other participants knowing their scores or even the instructor knowing the person's score. This capability enhances self-directed learning and measuring learning without imposing any feelings of inadequacy on the part of the learner.

   Thus, a daily quiz could be created by the instructor and participants could test their progress daily. Or potential participants in your online program could test themselves in advance of the program to see if the program material is too advanced, too elementary, or just right for them.

2. Instructors can gain access to a participant's test scores. If the test is set up so that the instructor can have access to the participant's test scores, then the instructor can aid the participant in his or her progress in the program. This would allow the instructor to provide specific recommendations for each learner.

3. Surveys can be conducted. Surveys can be taken on a daily basis and that information can aid in the instruction of online programs. Opinions, behavior, and other things can be surveyed and the results tallied and posted almost immediately, so that all participants can see the results.

Chapter 6
How Knowledge
is Organized Online

Not only is learning online a different experience, but knowledge is actually organized differently on the Internet. This new structuring of knowledge changes the way we as teachers construct content for our online courses.

Four new principles of how knowledge is organized online are:
1. Exploration of knowledge goes deeper, not down.
2. Knowledge content units or objects become reusable.
3. Original sources are accessed more for content.
4. Online courses become permanent, like a book.

There are several forces behind these changes. For one thing, there is a tremendous growth of knowledge and information. Today there is more information and knowledge than any one person, any group, any society, any organization could possibly acquire. And new knowledge and information is being created at a faster rate than ever before.

Adults over 40 grew up in a time when the amount of knowledge was more manageable, when one could start at the beginning and read to the end. So people growing up in the 20th century read left to right, top to bottom, start to finish. This is not how young people on the Internet read, says the father of a bright teenager interviewed by Margo Adler on National Public Radio. Because there is too much information, reading on the Internet becomes a process of discovery.

A second and related force affecting how knowledge is organized online is the growing specialization and segmentation of knowledge and information.

How information is organized on a web site

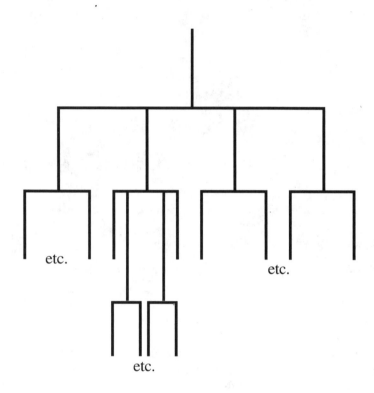

How information is organized on a web site.

New jobs are being created every day. New disciplines, subdisciplines, and areas of study are being created every day.

To cope, people in the workforce concentrate or focus on increasingly smaller areas of knowledge, or specialties. And people are segmented into narrower and narrower interest groups.

This increasing specialization means that one can take a course and divide it up into ten different parts and offer a whole course on each of the ten different parts. And then one can take each of the ten different parts, divide them again into subparts and offer a whole course on each of the one hundred subparts.

With so much information, so specialized, and changing so quickly, the Internet is becoming the primary source of information and cognitive knowledge. The Internet can store all this information, it can be updated, and it can be delivered instantly to anyone and everyone.

Make Text Readable

Make your online text readability. Not only look at different fonts and font size, but also look at white space and at color to make online text more readable. — Julie Rorabaugh, Butler Community College, Wichita, KS

How Information is Organized on a Web Site

Information on a web site is organized like a complicated set of ladders, where you start at the top and go "deeper," choosing which ladder you want to use next. It is the very same method that students used to use to outline a report. The outline went like this:

I. xxxx
II. xxxx
   A. xxxx
   B. xxxxx
     1. xxxx
     2. xxxx
       a) xxxx
       b) xxxx, etc.

All items with the same type of designation (I, II, III, etc., A, B, C, etc.) have roughly equivalent importance and are distinct from each other. When items appear indented within a larger category (for example, B., followed by 1.2.) that means the items are within the same general cat-

How we organize knowledge is changing.

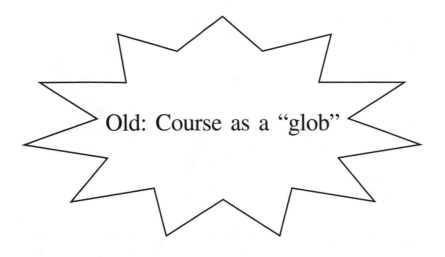

We used to think of a "course" as a single entity, a big 'glob.'

egory and are subtopics or specialized information.

This is how web sites are organized. My master web developer, Cem Erdem, designed a web site schema for me this way:

Home Page

I	II	III
A. B.		A. B. C.
1. 2.		1. 2. 3.
a) b) c) etc.		

IA.2.c) would probably be something more in-depth and specific in the whole area of whatever information I,A is about. A screen of copy for IA.2.c) would be "deeper" than I or IIIB., for example. IA. and IB. would be more closely related in subject matter than IB. and IIIB., for instance.

Later we will discuss how this organization of web site design impacts your learning online.

Course Information is Organized Differently

Course information is also being organized differently. Susan Kirshbaum, head of online learning products for Oracle, a large software company involved with storing data and information, says that a course used to be thought of as a single identity, a huge "glob" as she calls it. Adds Guenther Weydauer, Vice President for New Product Development at LearningByte International, a content development company, "the worst kind of course content architecture is a bunch of HTML documents thrown together."

That is changing.

Knowledge is being broken apart and broken down. The once-whole glob course is now composed of units or modules or lessons. Each unit is a separate entity, with a separate focus or theme or set of concepts or skills. Taken together the units make up a course. Broken down, each unit is itself an interesting, almost-independent entity.

Units can be broken down further into subunits. A subunit might be a page of copy, on which there is a single central thought or idea. Subunits are arranged in a way that makes sense and compose a unit. But subunits might be broken apart and each might be used again in a different course.

Here's how it breaks down:

• Curriculum (a set of related courses that compose the entire study)

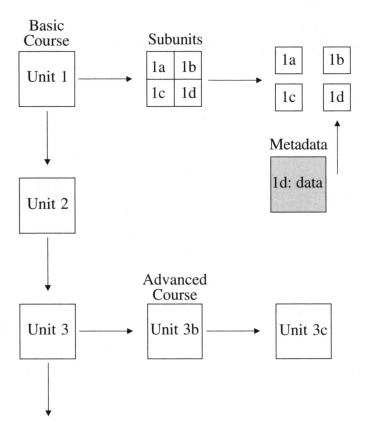

Online knowledge is organized by units or modules, and then broken up into even smaller subunits.

- Course (a complete course of study, with a beginning and an end)
- Units (from 5 to 15 independent and different lessons, each with a different focus or theme)
- Subunits (a smaller breakdown of knowledge with a single focus or concept)

Reusable Data

Instead of creating, rewriting, and reinventing pieces of data or knowledge, eventually researchers, authors, professors and others (including maybe you) will create subunits of knowledge or information.

Open Up Your Information

Open up your information. Everyone should receive information. Develop a checklist for administration, learners, and teachers, such as when notifications about a given event or procedure went out. Communicate with everyone. — Teresa A. Etter

---

Then anytime someone wants to use that subunit of information in a course, the information is available and can be used (probably for a price, but probably a pretty small price). Several benefits will then accrue.

- The best information and knowledge is available and widely used.
- It doesn't have to be recreated time and time again.
- It is presented in its best form, illustrated and conveyed in the best possible manner for maximum understanding and learning.

Weydauer says that the reusable units of data are organized into "shareable content objects," or SCOs. A shareable content object is content that is reusable and shareable, that is, can be used at different times in different courses sponsored by various institutions or providers.

According to Weydauer, a SCO:

- is 10-20 minutes of learning (in written, audio, video or other form).
- has 5-15 learning interactions taking place within it.
- satisfies a small number of learning objectives.
- has an inter-operability connector which allows others to access the SCO.

An agency in the defense department of the United States government is heading up an effort to develop an industry-wide standard for shareable content objects. The specification's initials are SCORM.

How the Discovery Method Works

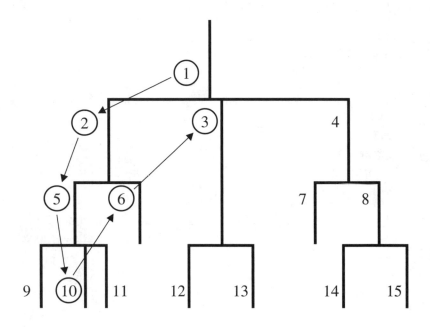

Using the discovery method online looks like aimless "surfing" but when you diagram how someone might move from page to page on a web site, it makes sense.

The Creation of Metadata

To help find, access, and determine the relevance of reusable data, a new kind of data has been created. This is data about data. It is called "metadata." This data might be hidden, or be visible, but it tells a person what the subunit or data is about.

Weydauer says that metadata act like "a card catalog in a library." For instance, it could convey:

- what you should learn first if you don't understand this subunit or data.
- what you should learn next if you do understand this subunit or data.
- what other subunits or data this piece of data is related to.
- what kinds of people (jobs, industries, interest areas) might be interested in this subunit or data.
- what kinds of courses this subunit or data might be used for.

Credibility Statements Stem Plagiarism

I require my students to turn in a "credibility statement" for each source that they use in their research papers. UCLA's library offers online several resources for students to use in developing credibility statements. These have kept the students focused on the fact that I (or my student assistant) check their sources; I haven't seen evidence of plagiarism since I started requiring the credibility statements. Also, the credibility statements are a great teaching tool. Try www.ucla.edu and link to the library resources page. — Tom Lewis, Liberal, KS

Aiding in the creation of metadata is XML, or Extensible Mark-up Language, which has some advantages over HTML, or HyperText Mark-up Language. These new "set of tags on language" will make it easier to tag data in a variety of formats and delivery systems.

An Example

Putting the concepts of subunits, reusable data, and metadata together, here is an illustration of how this will be used in practice.

Let's create two different online courses:

The History of Baseball

The History of Race Relations

Here's a sample of the outline for the History of Baseball:
The Invention of Baseball
The Early Years
The Black Sox Scandal
Babe Ruth
Jackie Robinson and the Color Barrier
The Yankees
Baseball Today, and so on

Here's a sample of the outline for the History of Race Relations:
Slavery in America
The Civil War
Race Relations in the Early 20th Century
Eleanor Roosevelt and World War II
Jackie Robinson and the Color Barrier
The Civil Rights Movement
Race Relations Today, and so on

A Reference for Chunked Copy

A good reference for writing chunked copy for the web comes from Jacob Nielsen at http://www.useit.com/papers/webwriting/writing.html. His main theme is scannability for web readers.
— John Brooks, Central Community College, Grand Island, NE

Did you see "Jackie Robinson and the Color Barrier" in both courses? This is an example of a unit that could be used in both courses. This unit could have the foremost authority on Jackie Robinson compose and write it. There could be interviews with his children or grandchildren. There could be photos and film and audio. It could be the best and most complete narration and elucidation about Jackie Robinson and his impact on the color barrier. It can be used again and again. And since it is the best, it is the best subunit for you and me to learn from.

This is an illustration of how subunits, reusable data, and metadata will be used in online learning.

Original Sources are Accessed More
As a result of the ability to create reusable SCOs and find them with metadata, one of the trends we are likely to see in the next few years is that original sources will be accessed more for content.

Instead of having an instructor talk about a prize-winning poem, for example, the class will be able to access the poet talking about the poem. There are at least two implications for you in developing your online course. One is to look for opportunities to access existing content. Look for high quality content that already exists and thus reduces the amount of work or rework you have to do in developing your online course content. Secondly, look for original content in your own work which might become a shareable content object at some point. Original work online no longer has to be a book or a course; it can be a much smaller unit of knowledge.

Online Courses are Permanent

This new way of organizing knowledge on the Internet, and of shareable content objects, reusable data, and metadata, has changed the nature of courses and classes.

"All teaching becomes publishing," notes a copyright and intellectual property expert at a recent education conference. "Every class is now a published work."

So your online course is a digitally-fixed or permanent entity, unlike face-to-face classes which were transient and 'disappeared' after being offered. Your online course can be accessed before, during, and after the actual time of offering. The interactions and dialogue in the class become a permanent record. And your permanent online course now can easily be analyzed, compared and contrasted to other "published" online courses.

This is a fundamentally new way of approaching the development of a course, and it offers exciting possibilities for enhancing quality and serving students better.

Chapter 7
Copyright and
Intellectual Property Issues

Intellectual property and copyright issues related to online courses are complex, controversial, and present new challenges to everyone in education, noted a panel on the topic at a recent international education conference in Vancouver.

And in their latest book, Palloff and Pratt make copyright and intellectual property issues on of the top issues in online learning.

At the time of this writing, copyright and intellectual property issues are an area where there are few answers, where the lines drawn are vague and often changing, and where it is unclear whether the standards and laws of the Industrial Age apply to the Information Age. Copyright and intellectual property issues are one of the top interest areas for online teachers. They are also issues of high concern for leaders in business, government and law. In one sense, copyright and intellectual property issues go to the core of what the Information Age, including education and online learning, is all about in the 21st century.

There are at least three fundamental questions related to copyright and intellectual property:

1. What and how much material from another source can a teacher use in an online course?
2. Who owns the online course, the teacher or the institution providing it?
3. What are the intellectual property issues of marketing and selling content and online courses to others?

There are no clear answers or consensus on any of these issues.

The following was not written by a lawyer and does not in any way constitute legal advice. Consult your attorney for any legal advice. It is provided for information purposes only.

There are at least three aspects to these issues, according to a panel of copyright and intellectual property experts:

- Legal aspects. Consider what the state, government and the courts allow, protect, and leave unprotected.
- Economic aspects. Consider what commercial potential exists, what demand there is, and whether the content is affordable.
- Moral rights. Consider to what information and content the public, nonprofits, teachers and learners have a moral or ethical right.

Contracts

One of the suggestions that arose from the discussions with my students was for group members to develop a binding learning contract based on a script provided by the instructor at the beginning of the semester. The purposes of such a contract are to establish common behavior guidelines, establish interaction and communication protocols, identify member roles, and develop contingency plans. We've been doing contracts in my class ever since! — Karen Murphy, Texas A&M University, Bryant Station, TX

Using Other Material

Most U.S. copyright law applies to non-digital environment, but there are some interesting possible implications for digital copyright law.

Section 110(1) says that material can be used in educational courses in face-to-face classes. Section 110(2) indicates that material that is not a play or movie can be displayed in a course, but not reproduced. And the Fair Use Section 107 says that teaching clearly qualifies under Fair Use.

A conference on fair use issued some controversial guidelines in 1997, which received little support.

In an interesting case, *Chavez v. Arte Publico Press* (204F.3d.601, 5th Circuit 2000), the University of Houston was found immune from a copyright infringement claim because it was an entity of the state, and states are exempt under sovereign immunity.

And Senators Hatch and Leahy introduced a Technology Education & Copyright Harmonization Act in March 2001, to try to resolve some of these issues.

Fair Use Guidelines for Educational Multimedia

Fair Use Guidelines for Educational Multimedia are a set of guidelines for educators, including educators working in an online environment. Ko and Rossen note, "They are guidelines rather than legal code because no formal amendment to the basic copyright law has been adopted. Nevertheless, an educator adhering to the Fair Use Guidelines is probably immune from liability in a suit."

Several considerations should be taken into account, including:

- Commercial versus noncommercial use. Teaching is noncommercial, and thus much less a problem. If you were to use material for a commercial use, then unauthorized use would be more of a problem.
- Original versus factual. One is less likely to encounter problems using material which is either factual or in the public domain. But original or creative work, especially if it is not in the public domain, is more likely to require permission for use.
- A lot versus a little. If you use a little information from another source, you are less likely to encounter a problem. If you use a lot of information or material from another source, there is more likely to be an issue with permission.
- Financial harm versus little impact. If your use causes the owner of the material little or no financial impact or loss of income, there is less of a problem. If your use denies the owner of the material financial gain or income, there is more of an issue.

The web site of the Fair Use Guidelines for Educational Multimedia offers these highlights and details:

- Beware license agreements. They may negate parts of fair use.
- The Guidelines apply to fair use for educational and scholarly uses of education multimedia projects only. They do not cover commercial projects for which you will need to get permission.
- The Guidelines apply to the use, without having to ask permission, of lawfully acquired copyrighted works (that means no illegal, pirated, or off-air copies, etc.) in educational multimedia projects which are created by educators or students as part of a learning activity by nonprofit educational institutions.
- Teachers creating teaching tools in support of a class at educational institutions fall under the Guidelines. Teachers may also incorporate their own material in with the copyrighted items.
- Guidelines support asynchronous distance learning if:

1. The network is secure;
2. The material can be password protected;
3. The technology can restrict the ability of making a copy.

- If copies cannot be restricted but the network is secure, a multimedia educational project can only be used for 15 days after its initial use in class or 15 days after its assignment for self study. After the 15 days, a copy may be put on reserve in the library for on-site use only.
- Teachers may show their multimedia projects at workshops and conferences and may include them in their personal portfolios.
- Time Limitations: if the network is secure and copies cannot be made, the project can be used for two years after its first use in class. After that, permission is needed.
- Portion Limitations: How much can I use? (The figures below imply whichever is less.)
    1. Motion media. 10% or 3 minutes, whichever is less.
    2. Text. 10% or 1,000 words, whichever is less.
    3. Music, Lyrics, and Music Video. 10% but no more than 30 seconds from an individual work.
    4. Illustrations and Photographs. Hard, because fair use usually precludes the use of an entire work. May use in one educational multimedia work: no more than 5 images by a single artist or photographer; no more than 10% or 15 images from a published collective work.
    5. Numerical data sets. 10% or 2,500 fields or cell entries from a copyrighted database or data table.
- Copying and Distribution Limitations: No more than two use copies, one of which may be placed on reserve. One copy may be made for preservation.
- Attribution and Acknowledgment: It is good form to credit sources and display the copyright notice and ownership information. Include author, title, publisher, place and date of publication. Copyright should show ©, year of first publication and name of copyright holder. Credits may be shown separately but graphics credits must be displayed with the graphic unless, such as in the case of an art class, this would defeat the educational objective.
- Alterations: Alterations to copyrighted works incorporated in educational multimedia projects may be made only if the alterations support specific instructional objectives. It should be noted that alterations have been made.

Online instructors often do the following:
* Wherever possible, seek or confirm permission. This is easiest done with e-mail. If no one responds, you at least have a record of your request.
* Consult your institution's policies and legal counsel.
* Pay royalties where that is clearly the law.
* Follow the established Fair Use guidelines.
* Serve your students' learning interests.

Who Owns an Online Course?

Another of the top issues among online teachers is who owns the online course, the teacher or the institution sponsoring it.

The short answer, and the correct answer, is whatever agreement you make with your institution.

Here are some thoughts about negotiating with your institution or host provider:
* Request a nonexclusive clause. Seek a clause of nonexclusivity so that you can teach another course, or even the same course, at other institutions. I am familiar with at least one instructor who teaches online for her own institution in Michigan, and teaches the same course online for two other universities in California. I know of at least one professor who co-teaches on online course with another institution.
* Clarify the agreement length. Clarify whether the agreement is for the life of your employment with the institution, or whether the online teaching portion of your contract can expire, and thus be renegotiated, after two to three years.
* Determine who owns it. Determine who owns it, and whether "it" is the course, or content, or learning objects used in the course. Your institution may have a standard agreement. However, these are unusual times, and you can be entrepreneurial in your approach. You can try to negotiate certain provisions. You can find out what your options relative to teaching in-person, teaching online for another institution or provider, and developing content on your own.

Who Should Own It

The issue of who "should" own your online course, or content, or shareable content objects (SCOs), is a matter of much discussion, debate, and no clear answers.

It is often linked with the issue of whether or not you will be paid for the development of the online course. Using that schema, there are four alternatives:

1. You use your own time to develop the course, and you own it (reasonable).
2. You get paid to develop the course, and the institution owns it (reasonable).
3. You use your own time to develop the course, and the institution owns it (not in your best interest).
4. You get paid to develop the course, and you own it (not in the institution's best interest).

There are incidences of all four alternative ownership plans. At the time of this writing, there is no clear front runner.

Contract Contents

I prompt my small groups with ideas to include in their learning contracts, things like:
- Who will be the group leader? Or will this task be rotated?
- Who will be responsible to post a given assignment?
- How will absences, failures to meet obligations, or other conflict be resolved within the group? — Mary I. Dereshiwsky, PhD, Northern Arizona University, Flagstaff, AZ

This online teacher's own prediction, and recommendation, is that the ownership of an online course look very much like the ownership of a book, only with a time limit associated to it. That is, when an educator or anyone else authors a book, the writer uses his or her own time in the research and writing of the book, and then holds the copyright to the work. The author then engages a publisher, who has the exclusive rights to publish the book. Should the publisher cease printing the book or making it available, the rights for future publishing revert back to the author.

Mott Community College in Michigan has an arrangement by which the teacher owns the content, but the college owns the course. This may not differ in substance from the author/publisher model.

Another model being reported is that both teacher and institution have ownership rights, so that the teacher can take the course somewhere else, but the institution can also continue the course should the teacher (and course developer) leave.

Adding to this issue is whether the teacher is acting as an independent agent, or being contracted by the college, or is acting as an employee.

Economics Different

The Italian Publishing Association and Department of Economics at the University of Bologna, the world's oldest university, are also working on a copyright standard.

There are economic issues involved, according to Piero Attanasio. He says:

- In a F2F course, the fixed costs are low (writing lecture notes) while the variable costs (giving the lecture over and over again) are high.
- In an online course, the fixed costs are high (creating online content) while the variable costs (offering the course) are low.

Additionally, if there is multimedia with many contract providers involved, the transactional costs increase for the course provider.

Marketing Online Content

A third related issue about copyright and intellectual property involves ownership with the intent to market or sell that content online.

Here's the dilemma in brief: If you own the content, I want to use it for free. If I own the content, I want to charge you to use it.

On the one side, corporations want to own information (intellectual property), have exclusive right over its distribution, and be able to charge others for using that intellectual property. Corporations are trying numerous methods to accomplish this goal, including writing encryption codes, proposing laws, seeking economic sanctions, creating industry-wide standards, and more.

Corporations are currently fairly adamant about this. "This whole concept of intellectual-property creation and being able to protect content or intellectual property is key," Intel chairman Craig R. Barrett noted in an interview with the *New York Times*. "If you don't have the ability to protect that which you create, society falls apart."

Walter Stewart, an executive with SGI, helped explain the private sector's keen interest in intellectual property. He says that in the Industrial Age, companies made money by making things. But in the 21st century companies are finding it harder to make money by making things. Thus, in the Information Age and our new knowledge economy, business is turning to producing information, knowledge, even education.

On the other side, a generation of boys, entrepreneurs, individual and

59

civil rights advocates, academic freedom activists, and others would like intellectual property to be free and freely distributed.

They have been active as well. Web users have generally patronized web sites with free information, while those sites trying to sell information have had a more difficult time.

The most famous issue to date was Napster (1999-2003), software which provided people with the ability to download and play music, regardless of copyright. Napster lost in court and became a legitimate software provider, Apple began iTunes, and music effectively has moved from a tangible item (CDs, records, etc.) to an intangible item. Yet, at the time of this writing, other software programs have taken Napster's place and the issue of intellectual property and copyright control continues. According to Stephen Downes of the National Research Council of Canada, the users will win the issue and companies will find it hard to win the online content ownership battle.

Massachusetts Institute of Technology (MIT) announced it would make available hundreds of its courses and course material free over the Internet.

While companies are creating encryption codes and software to protect their intellectual property, students, professors and others are creating de-encryption codes and software shortly thereafter to negate the effectiveness of encryption.

The solution will have to be something that is economically sustainable, fair to users and the general public, legally enforceable, and morally and ethically acceptable to a majority of people.

One of the troublesome areas might be with "trade secrets." A trade secret is information that is not sold, but rather kept from the public. A company can buy the digital rights to content and then prevent others from having access to the content. Thus certain knowledge could be kept secret.

Educators such as yourself and educational institutions may be central to the resolution of this issue. Education is on both sides of the issue, wanting to use copyrighted material, and also engaged in producing it. Education serves the general public and has a mission to advocate for the educational interests of the majority of citizens in society. At the same time education works with business and the private sector. And education has as deep and serious a self-interest in the issue as any other party. Whatever solution is adopted, it will need to enhance and further education and learning, an essential ingredient in the "Information Age" of knowledge workers and lifelong learning.

—Greg Brecht

The Impact of SCOs

All three issues: using copyrighted material, course ownership, and marketing online content, may very well be impacted by the development of SCOs, or Shareable Content Objects.

Many online experts foresee the widespread use and acceptance of SCOs in the development of online courses. Courses may cease to be unified single entities and may become a package of SCOs. Researchers, authors and teachers may own SCOs rather than courses. And SCOs may exhibit their own economics, with some being free, others available for extremely low cost, and still others with a much higher price tag.

Chapter 8
Planning Your Online Course

Below are a variety of considerations and things to think about in planning your online course. You should use them as brainstorming items. Discard those items which are known or a given to you. Don't worry about those items for which you have no control, or don't have an answer.

And do not spend too much time in the planning phase before you begin actual development of your online course. For most activities, I recommend as much planning as possible. But for online courses, you should spend an appropriate amount of time, but then move directly into developing your online course. Do not dwell on these items. Do not try to make your first online course perfect; it won't be. Your expertise as an online instructor is greatly dependent on your experience. As soon as you feel ready to move ahead, or feel as though you are getting behind, move into the development phase.

Before you begin to develop your course, here are some planning items to think about.

Audience

Too often we as teachers assume we know who our participants will be, or we throw the doors wide open and indicate that anyone and everyone is welcome in our course.

The better online instructors try to determine who the audience will be, and then find out as much as possible about their online participants.

In college courses, for example, it is helpful to know the mix of age ranges, as you may have students from age 18 to senior citizens in your class.

Plan your course around the audience you will be serving.

Niche/Curriculum

Some instructors simply react and develop online courses based on current needs. The better online instructors try to develop an online course which will have a niche or fill a gap in a curriculum. By looking at the overall curriculum, you can plan your online course to establish a niche and meet a central need in the overall curriculum.

Long-term goal

Where do you want your online course to be in three years? Where do you want to be in terms of your scholarship, teaching and research in three years? Where will the market, need or your discipline or field be in three years?

Many teachers create online courses for a present need. The better online instructors look to a longer term goal both for their courses and for themselves professionally.

Calendar

A calendar is an excellent tool to help your students manage their work in your online course. Use the calendar for deadlines, notices of exams, changes, and instructions. Make your calendar open to students. When students have the ability to post on the class calendar, they use it more and will check it more often. Students can input their own small group activity deadlines, meetings and other functions. — Dr. Maria Bonilla-Romeu, Inter American University of Puerto Rico

Length of course

Teacher-mediated online courses range from a few days to six months. The length is dependent on your subject and on the needs, flexibility and schedule of your participants.

For a 3-credit online course, higher education online experts recommend 16 weeks, the same as a traditional classroom course. While a 16-week 3-credit course could be done in half the time, Dr. Rita-Marie Conrad of Florida State University says that after trying a shorter course, she moved back to 16 weeks because it gives students more reflective time.

Course price

If you are marketing your online course, price to your participants is an important consideration. In general, the lower the price the more the registrations. Unlike face-to-face education, customers to not perceive a higher value to a higher priced online course. At the time of this writing, online courses priced below $100 have much higher registrations than higher priced courses.

Student time expectations

Ballpark the amount of time you expect students to devote to your course. While some students will devote more, and some less, a rough average is helpful in determining the extensiveness and difficulty of your course.

For example, Dr. Conrad estimates that about 135 hours of student work goes into a typical three-credit college course.

Title

Even in formal education courses, the title of the course is important. The course title can stimulate more people to enroll in your course, and the course title also indicates the emphasis or focus of your particular course.

Promotion

If you're doing your online course for continuing education, training, or another setting in which someone will be marketing your course, you can help by thinking a bit about how your course will be promoted.

Finances

Find out how much expense money you have to develop your course. Determine how much time you can devote to your course for the amount of money you will be paid for teaching it. Find out if there are any ways you can assist in making your course as financially feasible as possible.

Team members

If you are developing your course with the assistance or involvement of others, think a bit about who your team members are and what their roles will be.

In their excellent book, *Faculty Guide for Moving Teaching and Learning to the Web*, Boettcher and Conrad talk about development teams and about delivery teams.

Development teams may involve an instructional designer, web designer, graphic artists, technical support, and project manager. A delivery team, say Boettcher and Conrad, may involve an assistant, web support person, technical support staff, and administrative coordinator.

Team teaching

A variety of models are developing for involving more than one teacher, expert or discussion facilitator in an online course.

A single teacher is probably the easiest way to proceed logistically, and it may save time if only one person is in charge of the course development.

Team teaching "presents some unique challenges," caution Ko and Rossen. Some online experts, such as Ko and Rossen, warn against team teaching for online classes with fewer than 15 students, while other on-line experts do not find problems with team teaching small classes.

A number of online courses have utilized the resources of an outside expert, author, faculty from another institution, or other "guest presenter" online. The guest presenter spends as little as one or two hours online interacting with students and presenting an added perspective.

When Development Time Becomes Enjoyable

One of the things that helps me in terms of the time commitment of courses and the lack of time as a teacher is that the technical material is really interesting. It actually does take a lot of time, but it is challenging. When my software doesn't perform, it is challenging to problem solve my way out of it. When it finally works, I get the same satisfaction there as I do when I read a great book. — Grace Epstein, Kentucky Wesleyan College, Owensboro, KY

Another interesting model is developing for leading online courses. A lead instructor develops the course and is the primary resource for subject matter content, while co-instructors facilitate online discussion and student assistance for smaller groups of students (5-30).

While this is similar to traditional university lecture courses, in an online course there are more options for enlisting co-instructors, including:

- Faculty from other colleges and universities;
- Graduate students;
- Practitioners in the field;
- Teachers who focus solely on being facilitators and helping students learn;
- Students who have taken the course previously;
- Students who are currently taking the course.

—Greg Brecht

Redesigning a course

If your online course is a redesign of a face-to-face course you have been teaching, Boettcher and Conrad note a "web based environment provides the opportunity to reassess the strengths and weaknesses of a course." In particular, they note "this is a good time to find ways to increase active student learning and collaboration."

Student management files

Your online classroom software may have a built in student management system. Even so, Ko and Rossen write, "We urge you to become familiar with your software in advance, so that you can exploit its capabilities and compensate for its shortcomings." If a student management system is not built into your software, you will want to think about what records you want to keep, and how to create a system for file management. Ko and Rossen suggest teachers "create folders for student work on your computer and make sure that you've set up folders for student assignments in your e-mail program."

There may be only 2-3 of the above considerations which demand some planning in your course. To reiterate, budget your planning time, don't worry about solving all the problems the first time, and do not delay too long in beginning to develop your online course, as you will learn much from the practical experience.

Part III.
Developing Your
Online Course

Chapter 9
A Ten-Step Model

Developing an online course is an exciting, challenging, and personally rewarding experience. Unlike face-to-face classes, online courses are completely developed before the course starts. To some first time online teachers, this may seem like more work than a face-to-face class. But Dr. Rita-Marie Conrad, one of the foremost authorities on online teaching, notes that the workload is distributed differently. All of the developmental work has to take place before the class even starts.

To reiterate, there are three major components to a typical online course:
* Content
* Interaction
* Assessment

In this section, I will give you a Ten-Step Model or outline for developing your online course, followed by chapters on each of the three major components.

A Ten-Step Model

Here is a ten-step model to follow in developing your online course.

Step One. Course Goals, Title, and Objectives

Define and state your overall course goal. If you are teaching outside of formal education, defining your audience at this point is important. Even if you are working within formal education, defining your audience will be helpful.

Select a title for your course.

Next write down the objectives, outcomes or knowledge skills you want your participants to have achieved at the end of the course.

Step Two. Select Your Readings

Next, select your printed readings for your online course. From our experience teaching online, and noting the experience of other online teachers, the importance of a written text or set of readings has become evident. There are at least three reasons for this:

1. Putting lots of reading and text online hinders learning. From the experience of thousands of online learners we know that it is difficult and ineffective for learners to read lots of screen text.
2. The printed text or readings are a valuable learning tool. A book or readings are portable, tangible, and currently are the most effective way for learners to read large amounts of material.
3. A book or textbook greatly reduces your development time as a teacher.

Within those readings, mark the pages or sections that are:

***   Critical. They must be read.

**   Important. They should be read.

*   Nice. They could be read.

Disability User Friendly

Search for "bobby" or "accessible web design" to help determine whether your online course is user friendly for students with disabilities. — Dale Anglada, Pace University, New York, NY

This will give your learners guidance to what you deem important. It will also give them the opportunity to pursue readings in those subject areas that are of particular interest to them. In the Information Age, the reality of the situation is that there is always more information to read than one can possibly read, no matter what the subject matter. This process also helps you determine what questions to put on quizzes and tests. Questions on tests should be covered in the readings that are Critical for your course.

Estimate the time it takes to read the critical sections or pages in the readings. This will assist you in realistically planning how much material can be covered. And it will inform your participants how much time they should plan to devote to reading.

A rough measurement for reading time is 20 pages an hour for nonfiction, 10 pages an hour for extremely technical information, and 40 pages an hour for fiction.

If you expect your participants to spend ten hours reading nonfiction material, then you can allocate 200 pages of reading in your Critical category.

You have chosen your course title, written your goals and objectives, and selected your textbook or set of readings. The next step is to create your modules or units.

Step Three. Create Units

Divide your course or topic up into five to fifteen 'modules' or units. An average number of units per online course is probably around ten. Each unit will be a separate, interrelated, component of the course.

Mid-semester Evaluation

Do a mid-semester online evaluation form for the course. This is not a mid-term test. It is an evaluation of the online course.
— Kristina Macmillan, Pace University, New York, NY

Each unit will have several knowledge skills or concepts associated with it. Each unit will have a given amount of text or reading. Each unit will have a separate discussion. Each unit will have a separate assessment or quiz function. Each unit will have a given time period or length of time during which you and your students are focused on that unit.

Illustration: Customer Service

As an illustration, if you were developing an online course in Customer Service, you might have these units:

1. Why customer service is important
2. Answering the telephone
3. Dealing with complaints
4. Responding to customer interest and inquiries
5. Writing correspondence to customers
6. Doing follow up contact with customers
7. Measuring satisfaction in customer service

Units can be sequential, beginning with the basics and then moving to more advanced information. Units can also be entities unto themselves. That is, a unit in your course could also be expanded and developed further into its own future advanced online course. Units should lead somewhere — horizontally to the next module, and/or vertically to

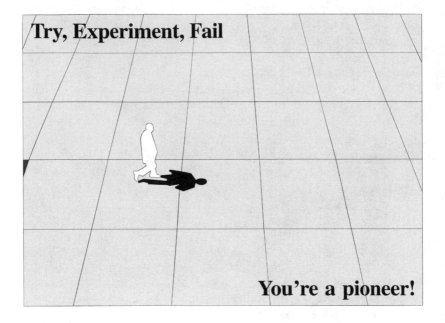

a more intensive and advanced set of units about the unit topic area. Units should also be able to stand-alone. That is, some of your learners will already possess the knowledge about a given unit.

This is where the importance of your textbook or set of readings becomes apparent. Ideally, the units of your course match up fairly well with the chapters in your textbook, or sections of your readings.

Subunits

At this point in time not many online instructors do a lot of work consciously dividing their units into subunits. But that will be coming. If you are an experienced online instructor, you might try dividing up your units into subunits to further your participants' mastery of different knowledge skills.

Frequent Initial Contact Enhances Retention

Right now I have 4 people participating in an online biology course. I have not yet tried to set up a discussion with this group. What can't be over-emphasized is the importance of contact in the first days of the course. Our college actually offers students a 10-day preview of the course before sign up During this time the student is contacted via e-mail by the program coordinator as well as the instructor and within the first two weeks the student also receives a phone call from the instructor. This has slowed the drop-out rate considerably.
— Sandy Sroba, Bow Valley College, Calgary, AB

Length of time

Units should be roughly equivalent in terms of length of time. That is, you would not want to spend one day on a given unit and then spend four weeks on the next unit.

For a three credit college course, for example, many units are one or two weeks in length. If you have a unit that is particularly short, you might consider combining it with another unit. If you have a unit that requires much more time, you might consider dividing it into two units.

As a practical matter, using weeks of time is a convenient and easily remembered way for your students to schedule their time and participate most actively. For that reason, one week is the most common length of time for a unit in an online course.

Step Four. Unit Content Development

For each unit, you will want to develop a set of competencies and outcomes, select readings, choose topics to be covered, and select online readings and links for further research.

Step 4a. Develop competencies and outcomes

For each unit, develop competencies and outcomes. These should be phrased in terms of knowledge concepts, skills, facts, or figures.

This goes hand-in-hand with the another step of developing your online course, designing online assessment.

Step 4b. Select unit readings

For each unit, select the readings in your textbook or set of readings that participants should read for each unit.

Step 4c. Select online readings

If there are short articles, new research, updated material or other concise readings that are available only online, or are best read online, include those for each unit.

Step 4d. Select links and references

If there are links to other web resources and references, include those for each unit.

Step 4e. Unit welcome pages

For each unit, you will want an introductory welcome page of announcements, notes, and directions. This will be the first online screen each participant sees for each unit.

Step Five. Unit Audio Presentations

Produce your audio presentations for each unit. You may have a varying number of audio presentations for each unit. The number of audio presentations does not have to be the same for each unit.

Step 5a. Script or notes

Write your audio script or do notes from which to speak.

Step 5b. Create PowerPoint visuals

For every 30 seconds to two minutes of audio, there should be a different PowerPoint slide to illustrate your presentation.

Step 5c. Record your unit lectures
Working with your technical person who will post or upload your audio files, record your unit lectures and submit your PowerPoint slides for synchronization.

Step Six. Unit Self-Assessment

For every unit, create one or more quizzes using your online classroom software. It may be a weekly quiz, or even a 1-3 question daily or subunit quiz. You as the online instructor may want to get the results. But the primary purpose of the unit self assessment quizzes should be as a learning tool to help your students understand their own mastery of the unit. In that sense, the self-assessment is not recorded for a grade but is purely a feedback tool to assist your participants.

Online Debate

For an anthropology course I taught, I divided the students into groups who then researched a specific topic. The fun part came when they were required to debate their group's standpoint online with the other groups. I conducted this type of debate three times over the semester.

The online debate was scheduled so all knew when to begin and when the end was. So, let's say the debate begins at 9 a.m. on Wednesday and ends at midnight on Friday. I limit the time frame for the debate because the number of messages can be large. I review the postings, strength of the argument, and the number of times each student posted and responded to others. I comment to keep focus on the debates, but also play devil's advocate to stir up controversy. This really gets them going. — Michael Phillips, Canton College of Technology, Canton, OH

Step Seven. Unit Interaction

For every unit, create one or more discussion questions or "rules" for online dialogue for you and your students.

Step Eight. Unit Projects, Exercises, and Activities

Depending on your course subject and audience, you may or may not want your participants to engage in projects, exercises, and activities.

Step Nine. Course Testing and Grades

For many online courses, grading and testing is determined less on a single test or paper, and more on a set of standards, including individual projects, online comments (both quantity and quality), online and offline tests, and papers, often involving peer review and/or collaboration.

You will first want to create your set of standards for a course grade, and then develop any final tests or exams.

Step Ten. Course Evaluation

Spend just a little time thinking about how you will evaluate your online course, and how you will want to gather and measure participant feedback, suggestions, and evaluations for your course.

Chapter 10
Building Online Content

For an effective online course, content is only one of three main components to your online course (the other two being Interaction and Assessment). Do not think of your course as merely delivering content online. As Conrad says, "Digital correspondence courses are in decline."

Nevertheless, content is a key element. As we gain greater expertise in teaching online, content will be delivered in ever-higher levels of sophistication, quality, interactivity, and multimedia. As increasing numbers of younger generations of 21st century students become online learners, the demand for quality, interactivity, and multimedia images in content will grow.

You can build online content in one or more of these ways:
1. Written online text
2. Visual graphic presentation
3. Virtual tours and WebQuests
4. Audio lectures
5. Video
6. Animation
7. Simulations
8. Music and sound clips
9. Drag and drop
10. Games
11. Gaming
12. Other variations and content delivery methods

Written Online Text

Written online text should not constitute the primary way you deliver content to your participants. A textbook or hard copy set of readings is better for large amounts of reading.

Online text is particularly useful for:

- short articles,
- new or updated material,
- material where there are accompanying links to other web sites, interaction, or accompanying visuals or simulations.

The overwhelming primary recommendation in writing online text is to "chunk your copy." Expert after expert repeat this phrase. It is still the single most important guiding principle.

Online text should be no longer than one or two screens in length. A learner should not have to scroll down the page. If that is happening, the copy is too long.

Music Online

I can ask students to listen to the bass line and know that retention is minimal. But with a file (online) I can isolate the bass line, or simply amplify it so it stands out, and have a pop-up appear when the song reaches the bridge, and so on. I'm very excited about this, because I believe it will make the music far more meaningful to motivated students. — Michael Campbell, Western Illinois University, Macomb, IL

Instead of scrolling down the page, provide links to the additional copy, taking your online learners "deeper" rather than "down." Think of your online text as a web site where the single entry page, or home page, leads to several more pages, and those pages have links to even more pages of information.

In this way, you can write more in-depth, intensive and comprehensive online text without straining your students' physical or mental capabilities.

The more visual, interactive, graphically-pleasing and linked the online text, the easier to read and the more interesting for your learners.

Visual Graphic Presentation

The more the better. Create pictures, graphs, charts, and other visuals online, accompanied by either text, or verbal presentation, or both. There is a variety of software available to help you create good visuals.

Think of the pictures as online overheads or slides. The best visuals are not merely words enlarged or put into color. The best visuals are usually true pictures or graphics.

There is a small but growing art and science of creating a new kind of visual which combines a picture with words to convey a concept better than either words or pictures could do alone. Julie Coates, Vice President of Information Services for the Learning Resources Network (LERN) is one pioneer in communicating in this form.

Think of different ways in which to create visuals, including:

- photographs
- drawings
- clip art and cartoons
- charts and graphs
- primitive line drawings
- demonstrations
- maps

We know that some kinds of students learn better visually. Visuals are not merely diversions or interest getters, they assist in the learning process.

Photographs and visual images are not merely "bells and whistles" for younger learners. They are an integral and essential learning mode. We have critiqued hundreds of online courses, and not found one that has too many photographs and visual images. Use as many photographs and visual images as possible.

Use more color

Too many online courses are colorless. Use more color on your web pages. Pay special attention to making that first 'home' page of your online course colorful and stimulating. If you can, ask the advice or assistance of someone from Generation Y on what colors to use, and how. Use colors your students appreciate.

Virtual Tours

Virtual tours are guided tours of other web sites where you as instructor create a "trip" to a series of web sites. You write an accompanying script to tell your participants what to look for and why the site is important or of interest.

Virtual tours are useful, and distinct from simply referencing URLS, in that they guide a student and also create a sequence that puts together knowledge and information.

Development Costs for an Online Course

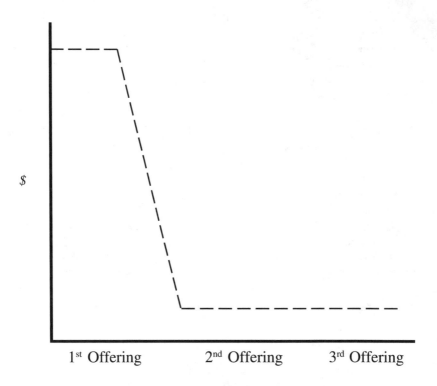

As the graph illustrates, content-rich online courses will have a high initial development cost, but very little cost after that. This is another reason why high volume, repeatable courses will be economically feasible online.

Virtual tours are a no-cost way to build content online and serve as an excellent learning resource and are recommended to you.

WebQuests

WebQuests are a marvelous educational aid involving using the web to help students explore and work with online projects. In a WebQuest the student is given a series of URLs on a specific topic, such as Mayan temples, and an assignment. The quest can be to visit specific web pages and gather specific information, or the teacher can more broadly define it with web sites and more flexibility and creativity in the assignment.

There are more than a thousand WebQuests already created and available on the web. You can create your own WebQuest as well.

Audio Presentation

Audio presentations online are effective, efficient for both teacher and student, help build community, help in the learning process, and enhance greatly the learning in your course. I strongly encourage you to integrate audio presentations into your online course.

You can do either real-time oral presentations, or prerecorded oral presentations. By far the more effective will be the prerecorded presentations, which have these advantages and characteristics:

- They allow you to present your best shot, both content and delivery-wise.
- You only have to deliver the information once. Thereafter, you can conserve your time and energy for interaction with your participants or developing new information and presentations.
- Your participants can listen to your presentation at their optimal time of the day.
- Your participants can review and re-listen to portions of your presentation.

After doing an audio presentation, develop a written table of contents for the presentation, much like songs on a CD. This highlights the primary concepts or points of your presentation, and it will tell the learner where in the presentation she or he can find each section of your talk. In this way, the learner can replay some portions that are more difficult or require extra attention on the part of the learner.

Illustration
   Handling Complaints (15 minutes total)
   :00   Introduction
   2:15   Hearing what the complainer has to say
   3:33   Six ways to express empathy
   7:48   Five steps to follow in handling the complaints
   11:03   Giving the complainer options
   14:17   Thanking the complainer
   14:48   Closing the conversation

As with your text presentations, chunk your audio presentations. Devote 5-20 minutes per audio presentation. The ideal length for an audio presentation seems to be 10-15 minutes.

In a section below, we explore in more detail both the technical aspects of putting audio presentations online, and the educational aspects of creating audio presentations.

Incorporating Math Symbols into Web Pages

1. Use MS Word to create your math pages, and then save them as HTML. Your math expression will be rendered as GIF files. 2. Use MS PowerPoint to do the same thing as in 1. This makes the math a little easier to read on the screen. 3. Produce your documents in a web-compatible program like Scientific Notebook or TI Interactive!. The drawback here is that the client must also have this software. — Don Davis, Lakeland Community College, Mentor, OH

Video

With more students having access to broadband connections, more online instructors have been incorporating video into the content of their online courses.

To be sure, for the majority of online instructors, audio with slides is the top priority concerning multi-media. Audio with slides is now a "must." Video is still an optional, though quality, multi-medium for those online courses where it makes sense. A few guidelines for video:

- Create video clips. Video should be chunked into clips that last anywhere from 30 seconds to a maximum of four minutes.

- Avoid the talking head. Video is not you as instructor being filmed while giving a lecture. That does not work visually or pedagogically.
- Capture motion or a scene. Video makes sense when it is either the best or only way to convey the message. Videos of demonstrations, machines in action, or wildlife are some examples where video is an excellent choice.

Use video judiciously, and make it of the highest possible quality.

Animation

Animation is here and it is being used by some. The best illustrations of animation online are short, maybe 30 seconds to 2 minutes long.

Some animations are cartoons which illustrate a point, technique, or concept. The Brain Pop animations at www.brainpop.com are an excellent example of this kind of animation.

Virtual Dissection

"Have you ever done a dissection virtually? I have the equipment (software) to do that and it is awesome, especially for the squeamish." — Katy Deffe, Great Falls, MT

Some animations are short moving picture clips illustrating a technique or activity, such as Ed Stephan's animations showing the baseball player Ted William's batting swing, or an animation showing the origin of motion pictures.

Some animations demonstrate how to do an activity, such as the great animations for tying different kinds of knots at one scouting web site. Ko and Rossen have the best references and URLs for animation examples.

If you are an experienced online teacher, consider incorporating an animation or two into your online course. Animations will become a common feature in online courses in the future.

Simulations

Simulations are animations with interactivity. They are commonly used in science courses, such as illustrating a chemical reaction, or how molecules interact, or how an engine works.

The first example of an online simulation I saw was in a presentation by Peter Cochrane of British Telecom at the University of Wisconsin distance learning and teaching conference. Cochrane showed molecules in a container, and then showed what happens to the molecules' motion and speed when the temperature is increased or decreased, and when more or fewer molecules are in the container. This amazing simulation illustrated a central advantage of online simulations: in many cases they are able to demonstrate something that cannot be as adequately demonstrated or shown in a physical laboratory.

More online teachers are becoming interested in developing visual interactive simulations on the web. These multimedia presentations involve motion, color, pictures and images, and sometimes audio. The best simulations are interactive, so that the student can manipulate processes or variables to redirect the simulation and discover the outcome.

Pollination of plants, dance techniques, molecules in a container, and the functions of a gas turbine engine are all examples of simulations. "Give the user as much control as possible," says online teacher Dr. Dan Lim of the University of Minnesota at Crookston.

Not every simulation has to be an original creation for every online teacher. Think about borrowing, sharing or collaborating with other online instructors in creating and utilizing simulations that can be shared.

Simulations are an example of the incredible potential of online courses. The simulations both involve the student in the demonstration, and also illustrate something that is more difficult to do in a physical setting.

Again, the vast majority of online teachers are not using simulations at the time of this writing, but they are likely to be a common feature in online courses in the future.

Music and Sound Clips

Music and sound clips are being used in a variety of ways in online courses. Music often can illustrate a point or concept better than words. Sound clips can be integrated into audio lectures, or used as separate references, providing original oratory or historical impressions. And some music, like the specially recorded music by the Lind Institute of San Francisco, create a background that enhances a person's receptivity to learning.

And music and sound can also be used to illustrate concepts. Michael Campbell, a music professor at Western Illinois University in Macomb, Illinois, for instance, explained to this author that he can dissect chords and certain parts of a score or music in order to focus on that particular aspect of the music. He can do this better, and with more variation, detail and effectiveness, online than he can do it in a face-to-face class.

There is an abundance of sources for music and sound clips for online courses. Some of it can be used using the Fair Use guidelines for music. Some music is copyright-free. And some music and sound clips can be used by paying a small royalty to the owner.

Music and sound clips are low cost and available. We know they enhance learning. I would encourage you to use them in both your audio lectures where relevant, and as separate files where appropriate.

Flash for Animations
For animations, use Flash and make them short. We do four animations in five minutes. — Karen Levy, Franklin University, Columbus, OH

Five sources of music

Here are five sources of music:

1. Use up to 29 seconds of copyrighted music for educational purposes under the Fair Use Guidelines (see Chapter 7)
2. Ask for usage of an original song from a relative, friend or kid.
3. Purchase a special CD composed, and advertised, of copyright-free music.
4. Ask a friend to play some music that is old enough that the copyright has expired.
5. E-mail a relatively unknown artist, or musician from another country, for the right to play their music in your online course and offer a donation or some other trade.

Drag and Drop

Drag-and-drop exercises are another excellent learning tool. In a drag-and-drop exercise, the student uses the cursor to move an online object around on the screen. The goal is to "drop" the object in the correct place. According to online expert Bill Horton, the physical movement involved in using the cursor increases the learning over simply reading or even listening about the subject matter. Examples of drag-and-drop exercises include puzzles, and placing countries in the correct geographic location.

Games

Games such as Jeopardy and crossword puzzles are another way to present content in a manner that is more involving to the learner, increasing retention. The University of Minnesota at Crookston, for example, has created a game site for any online instructor to use.

Gaming

"Gaming" is different from "games" in the online environment. Games could be Jeopardy or an online scavenger hunt. Gaming is a whole different world. Gaming involves your student interacting in a virtual world. Sometimes the world is a game, such as conquering an opponent. Sometimes the world is a cooperative creative environment, such as the medieval world of Evergreen. And sometimes the world is simply other people (their avatars actually) engaged in everyday activities, such as Second Life.

Probably the first course created entirely as a game is an education course developed by education professor Rod Riegle of Illinois State University. In professor Riegle's online game, there are no lectures, discussion, or tests. The entire course is the game. All information, communication and assessment is done in the game. Riegle says it took him ten years to create the online game/course.

For most faculty born before 1964, the gaming world will probably be very unfamiliar, strange and difficult. For most students born after 1980, gaming is a real, if virtual, world that teaches essential 21st century skills.

At the time of this edition, there were few gaming courses in schools and colleges. One of the big issues is the cost and time of developing a game to the level of sophistication necessary for today's students. Another major challenge is that many if not most teachers are not naturally inclined toward playing, much less creating, online games.

Gaming in education will become a significant learning strategy for generations of the 21st century. It is a growing and fascinating field. It is good for you to be open to online gaming and to understand what it is. You will see more teachers becoming in gaming every year.

And More

Variations of the above, as well as the possibility of new resources, are being created by online teachers such as yourself on an ongoing basis. The greater the variety in delivery, the more the learning is enhanced, the more you are able to respond to the different ways your students each learn, and the higher the quality and interactivity of your online course.

Development Time and Cost

One of the top questions teachers have about teaching online is the time and cost involved in developing the content of the online course.

If you are going to have a content-rich online course, initial development costs and time for the content aspect of your online course are high relative to the development cost of a face-to-face course. It does take a good deal of time to initially develop content. There may be costs involved. But if you have planned your course sufficiently, you should only experience this major development cost once per online course.

For a three-credit college course, the online experts I have interviewed indicate that it takes from three weeks to nine months to develop an online course. Boettcher and Conrad set the figure closer to nine months for a well-prepared and executed online course. A six-month cycle for planning and development is a reasonable amount of time. Less than three months would certainly be a "rush" job.

The amount of time within that time frame needed to develop an online course is harder to estimate, but 120 hours would have to be a minimum.

The cost of developing an online course has been estimated in terms of the range between $3,000 and $30,000. Much of the variability in this range is dependent on whether the developers of the course (you, and/or other subject matter specialists and your technical support staff), are being paid or costed out as a direct expense for online course development.

If your institution has the appropriate software and hardware, the vast majority of cost lies in your time.

Development Revisions and Updates

Conrad succinctly but eloquently states, "There is no such thing as a canned course. Every online course must be upgraded, and is changing and alive."

Indeed, after every time you offer your online course, you will want to make some changes, improve the quality, or create new features.

The amount of revisions, however, as well as the time and cost involved for those revisions, is up to much debate among online teachers.

Only a few teachers indicate that revisions take as much time as the initial course development, and this online teacher would maintain that there is some kind of weakness in planning an online course in which such major revisions are required.

More teachers would estimate that revisions account for about 5% to 10% of the original online course development.

With online course development, there is one major initial development time and cost incurred, and then subsequent revisions and updates require substantially less time and cost. This has been this online teacher's experience.

It has also been my experience that many revisions are improvements or additions to the course, increasing the quality of the course.

The best time to decide on your revisions for your next offering is right at the end of the current online course offering. The best way to proceed is to choose 1-3 revisions based on these criteria:

- Student input and feedback. Your students will point to the major weaknesses in your course from their standpoint.
- Centrality to the course content and student learning. There are numerous design and minor corrections that can be made to any course. Consider what revisions will substantially improve the course content and student learning.
- Feasibility. In terms of time and cost, what is feasible and realistic?

Choose only a few revisions each time based on the criteria above. Do not overload yourself with more work. If you want to try something new, take only one new risk each offering.

Work Time for Online Courses

One of the ongoing issues for online faculty is the issue of work and time devoted to online courses. What we can say for sure is that online courses, as well as the learning requirements of the 21st century, have changed the dynamics of your use of time as an instructor. Exactly what the ideal new time requirements should be is not yet clear. But here are some observations.

- Time spent in online discussion is good. Being engaged in online discussion is time well spent. Online discussion enables your students to learn more, be more involved, more motivated, more stimulated by your course. Devote as much time as you can to your online discussion.

- Development time is up front. The development time for your course is all before the course starts, so it "looks" and "feels" like you are spending more time. In reality, you are shifting your time.
- Time input is still the standard. Faculty members of the Baby Boomer generation (born 1946-1964) value time input from their students, and believe the more time spent, the better. Until this standard changes from time input to performance outcomes (what is learned) faculty will be in a double bind of requiring greater time input from students, then having to cope themselves with the same time constraints.
- We don't know how to save time. In general, adults are only beginning to discover ways in which to save time. From using software to changing lifestyle choices (such as where to live, or work), many adults have yet to implement time saving techniques in their daily work and personal lives. A National Center for Education Statistics study found that professors indicated they spend just 55% of their time teaching. One instructor negotiated with his administration to teach more classes provided he did not have to serve on any faculty committees. He was able to double his teaching load by eliminating committee time from his schedule.
- Student engagement can be win-win. Conrad and others suggest that engaging students in an increasing variety of class activities, from leading discussions to evaluating peers, is good pedagogy. It also saves faculty time. As more faculty engage students in more class activities and leadership, this represents a significant way in which good pedagogy supports saving faculty time.

Web Accessibility

You will want to make your course accessible to people with disabilities. Do a search for web accessibility or check out www.w3.org/WAI/ and trace.wisc.edu for a start. The w3 site, for instance, can help check your web pages to see if they are accessible, and will have links to other web sites on being accessible.

There are some general web design principles related to color and design to make your pages easier to read.

For the deaf and people with hearing disabilities, the most important thing to do is to provide a transcript for every audio message. A transcript is also a helpful learning aid for some people without hearing impairment, so the transcript serves two purposes. Next to each audio, have a link to a written copy of the audio script.

For the blind and people with visual disabilities, an important thing to do is to have ALT tags for each image or visual in your online course, say Alice Anderson and Blaire Bundy of the University of Wisconsin-Madison. People with a visual disability use a screen reader to read copy on the Internet. The screen reader converts the written word into verbal copy so the person hears the copy.

A screen reader such as JAWS cannot read an image, only words. When the screen reader encounters an image and there is an ALT tag on it, the screen reader then reads the copy on the ALT tag. The copy on the ALT tag describes the picture or visual.

Thus, when you have pictures or images in your online course, write short copy (256 characters maximum) for the ALT tag for each image, note Anderson and Bundy.

Bundy offers these guidelines for testing your online course for accessibility for the blind:

- Turn off the images on your browser.
- Turn your mouse upside down and don't use it. Use the tab keys to navigate the links.

He says that if you can navigate and read the copy without images and without using a mouse, that is the experience a blind person will have with your online course.

Another good technique, says Bundy, is to have someone with disabilities use your web site. Ask someone with a disability to check out your online course.

Chapter 11
Delivering Audio Presentations

Audio is becoming an integral part of online courses. We know that people learn in different ways. Some people learn by listening. And we know that learners each have a particular peak learning time. One of the advantages of recorded online audio is that each learner can listen at his or her own peak learning time, at his or her own speed, replaying some parts to reinforce their learning.

It is possible that recorded online audio presentations will make the traditional classroom lecture obsolete, and even replace live lectures in face-to-face classes, allowing both teacher and students to spend more time in discussion and on advanced topics or in-depth study.

For you as instructor, there are some things you can do with your voice that cannot be accomplished in other ways.

With audio, you teach in two ways. You teach by what you say, and you also teach by how you say it. Your tone of voice can induce enthusiasm, passion, concern, understanding, reassurance, confidence, conviction, motivation and encouragement.

You may start creating audio presentations by redelivering your in-person lectures, and that is fine. But you will then move beyond replicating in-person lectures, and begin to see online recorded audio presentations as having many more possibilities.

How Streaming Audio Works

by John Allen, Senior Technology Manager, LERN

Streaming is a method of delivering audio (or video) to your computer, or other capable device. Streaming differs from the "normal" method of listening to audio in one important way: instead of having to download an audio file, be it a .wav, .au, or other type of file before being able to listen to it, you hear the sound *as it arrives* at your computer. This method of delivery allows large files to be incrementally delivered to you, piece-by-piece. A sample file of music containing 57 seconds of music could yield a file as large as 9MB, which would take approximately 24 minutes to download over a 56K modem. With steaming (in Real format) that same file would take only 22 seconds to download.

However, since you are not downloading the file, the time it takes you to retrieve the file and listen to it in its entirety, is 57 seconds.

Virtual Spring Break

Virtual spring break. Create one and share as an online community. — Diana Wenzel, Township High School 214, Arlington Heights, IL

Why is there such a difference?

With a downloaded file, you must retrieve 100% of the file all at once, and then listen to it. With streaming, as the data arrives it is buffered for a few seconds and then playback begins. As the audio is playing, more data is constantly arriving (or streaming), and as long as you are receiving a constant stream of data, you should hear constant audio.

Think of a bucket (the buffer) with a hole in the bottom, being topped up with water (the data). As long as there is water in the bucket, it will continue to pour out of the hole. Similarly, as long as there is data in the buffer, you will continue to hear sound.

Keep in mind that you will need a server capable of streaming audio. Real, Microsoft, Apple and other software providers make these types of servers.

There are four necessary components to delivering streaming media.

1. Web server. This can be any regular web server and will typically have all of the front-end files that use streamed media. It stores and serves all associated text files that point to encoded video/audio files.
2. Web client software, a.k.a. browser. This is software on the client computer that accesses the web.
3. Streaming server. The streaming server is a dedicated server with streaming software to serve the encoded video/audio files. It will allow the multiple streaming of media files and access to any portion of any encoded file.

4. Streaming media client software. This software is launched by the web browser and runs as an external application to play and manage streaming files.

The typical delivery of streaming media goes something like this:

Step 1
All web pages are stored on special servers called web servers. When you click on a link in a web page to listen to a clip (whether live or pre-recorded) the web server sends your browser a small pointer file that is associated with that link.

Step 2
Your browser recognizes that the file isn't just another page so it checks to see what program can read it. When it recognizes that it is a streaming file, it starts up your streaming media client software and passes the file off to the program.

Steps 3 and 4
The file is very small and contains only the name and location of the clip on a streaming server. Your streaming media client software contacts the server, which sends the actual stream, and then stays in contact with server so you can fast forward or rewind or otherwise navigate through the clip. In the case of channels and live stations, streaming media client software speaks directly to the streaming server without the need for the earlier pointer file. Streaming servers are similar to web servers but rather than serving pages to browsers, they serve streams to streaming media client software. Streaming servers work in concert with web servers to bring multi-media to networked environments, such as the Internet.

Creating Audio Presentations

One of the areas online teaching pioneers are exploring is what should be said in an online presentation.

There are several different approaches and kinds of material that can be delivered in audio presentations:

New material and updates
Since the publishing date of the text for your course, there may be new material and updates which can be talked about in your audio lecture.

There might also be some information you deem important which was not covered in the text, and that can be incorporated into your audio.

Anecdotes, examples, illustrations

Your audio lecture can complement the text, providing anecdotes, examples and illustrations that are not in the text, come from your personal experience, or are better delivered by listening rather than reading.

Your perspective

As teacher, you may want to add your own perspective, research or opinions to the information your class participants receive. Your audio lecture is a way for you to do that.

Summary of important points

You can use your audio lecture to summarize the important points in the readings and in the course, using it as a verbal underlining so your students understand what you deem to be most important.

Emphasize certain information

You could also use your audio lecture to emphasize certain information or aspects, spend more time where you think it is warranted, or go more in-depth on certain topics.

Pep talk or instructions

Your audio lecture may also be a pep talk, a motivational and emotional stimulus for your participants. We know that learning is not simply cognitive, that learning involves emotions. So this is a legitimate use of an audio lecture.

Or you may use your audio lecture to underscore your instructions to the class. "Here's what I want you to do..." "I want you to..." can come across as a personal, positive encouraging pitch when delivered verbally to your class. In the 1930s the U.S. president Franklin D. Roosevelt used his radio fireside chats both as a pep talk and to give his nation instructions. Many of those listeners felt as though he was talking to them personally and individually.

Quotes and excerpts from others

Quotes and excerpts from other authorities often reinforce or add new perspective and insight to the course, and incorporating them into your audio lectures is a valuable approach.

Storytelling

Storytelling may be one of the most effective uses of audio lectures, as many stories are better told than read.

The great 20th century short story writer Eudora Welty (for whom the popular e-mail program was named), provides a clue as to why stories are well received, and also how to begin to create your own stories:

"Long before I wrote stories, I listened for stories. Listening 'for' them is something more acute than listening 'to' them. I suppose it's an early form of participation in what goes on. Listening children know stories are there. When their elders sit and begin, children are just waiting and hoping for one to come out, like a mouse from its hole."

How to Record Audio Lectures

Here are some tips on how to create your audio lectures.

Length

Audio lectures should be "chunked" like online text, which means each audio segment should be short. Most experts recommend a range from 5 minutes to 20 minutes in length. The ideal length is 10-15 minutes.

Thus, instead of doing an hour lecture, you break up your hour lecture into six ten minute audio segments.

You will also find that an online recorded audio lecture compresses your live lectures, and that you can get the same amount of information in about half the time using a recorded online lecture. So your hour lecture might very well be accomplished in 3 ten-minute online lectures.

Script or notes

Online teaching experts differ on whether it is better to speak more extemporaneously from notes, or to use a written script.

The advantages of using notes are that your presentation comes off more informal, less rigid or forced, the language is conversational and more natural to speaking. The disadvantages are that you will have more wasted words, some "ums" and "ahs," it will be harder to slot the slides in appropriate intervals, and harder to stick to a prescribed time limit. So it is "looser."

The advantages of using a script are that you can compress more information into the time, waste not a single sentence, make sure you include all your points, stick to your time limit, and you can work the script so that your slides rotate at regular intervals, providing ongoing

An early version of the software for a Real audio player (circa 2002), it nevertheless is a good visual demonstration of the characteristics and capabilities of audio software. Note:
  - *in the lower right-hand corner the player tells you how long the audio lecture is (right of the slash) and where the listener is currently (left of the slash).*
  - *the bar near the top, below "Presets," can be moved with the cursor forward or backwards, so the listener can skip sections, replay sections, and thus use the listening time to best advantage.*
  - *the box on the right, with the Real logo, is where PowerPoint slides or other visuals appear, supplementing the audio.*

visual stimulation. The disadvantage to reading a script is that most of us read the script in a more rigid, less emotive, and less conversational manner and tone.

You pick whatever works for you. This online instructor began with notes, moved to a script, and is now working on reading that script in a more conversational, emotive, style.

Transcript

Whether you use a script or not, there are two reasons why an accompanying transcript of your audio lecture is helpful. One reason is that learners often like to refer to the written copy of your audio presentation, as it is a learning tool, even just checking on the spelling of a particular term. Another reason is that hearing impaired people can use the transcript to receive your audio lectures. Your transcript can be a simple posting of the copy of your lecture.

Structure

In each 10-15 minute audio segment, I would suggest:

- *A title*. It is good to have a title for each audio segment or file. This helps your participants focus on the topic.
- *Theme*. Concentrate on 1-4 concepts in each audio segment.
- *Summary*. For many lectures, an effective learning device is to state at the beginning what you are going to talk about and then summarize or reiterate those major points at the end of the audio segment for reinforcement.
- *Break*. This online lecturer has a 30-60 second break in the middle of each audio segment, often accompanied by music. The break allows my learners a little time for reflection. It signals that I will be transitioning into another concept or major point. And it helps maintain attention by telling the listener that we are half-way through the audio segment.
- *Three to five teaching techniques*. As you become more accomplished and experienced in delivering online lectures, you will want to incorporate 3-5 different teaching techniques in each audio segment.

Teaching Techniques

As in effective face-to-face lectures, you will want to incorporate 3-5 different teaching techniques into your online lectures.

In the section above, a number of different approaches to what to say all constitute different teaching techniques. So you can use this list as options.

In addition, you can use these additional teaching techniques to enhance your students' learning:

- Skits and role play. Using one or more colleagues or students, you can create simple little skits or role plays to convey concepts or points.
- Humor. In written online conversation or text, humor is difficult to convey. When you are speaking, it is easier to use humor as a teaching technique. Humor is not necessarily jokes or funny stories; it can also be a smile, upbeat enthusiasm, and friendly inflection in your voice.
- Music. Music is a powerful learning tool that can now be used much more easily and frequently when teaching online. Use music excerpts following appropriate copyright and usage guidelines.
- Poetry. Probably the most underused teaching technique, there are poems or at least rhythmically pleasing prose that address a wide variety of topics and subjects. Poetry is a wonderful verbal learning aid.

Synchronized Slides and Visuals

You can deliver audio lectures simply as audio, without accompanying slides or visuals. Such was this teacher's first experience with online lectures. But there is an enormous benefit of an accompanying visual stimulation as a learning tool and to maintain attention during the audio lecture. And slide shows are so easy to produce, and so well known to many of us as PowerPoint presentations, that logistically it is feasible and very low cost to add this beneficial feature to your audio lectures.

Synchronized slides do not take up much bandwidth and can be received well with simple telephone Internet connections. Thus, your students can readily access and receive your audio lecture with synchronized slides without normal interruption, connection or downloading problems. They do not need any additional software or plug-ins to receive synchronized slides with your audio lecture.

Synchronized means that the slides rotate or change automatically. You or your techie can set each slide to change at whatever interval or point in your lecture you wish.

The slide presentation can be done with PowerPoint or another slide presention software. Because so many of us are familiar with PowerPoint and have that software already available, I will refer to the accompanying slide presentation as a PowerPoint presentation.

Where to start

You can develop your audio lecture first and then develop an accompanying PowerPoint presentation to go with it, according to Les Howles of the University of Wisconsin, one of the nation's foremost authorities on synchronizing audio and slides.

For some subjects, says Howles, you will want to start with your PowerPoint slides and then develop your audio lecture around your slide presentation. And for still other situations, you may want to develop them together, going back and forth, working and reworking the presentation with the interplay of slides and script.

Make them visual

The primary consideration is to make your slides visual and graphic, not merely words on a background. Putting words on a background is probably the most common mistake. Use pictures, graphics, clip art, demonstrations, but avoid having all your slides be words on a background.

When you do use words, try incorporating pictures and artwork in with the words.

Intervals

At this time, an appropriate interval time between slides is 20 to 60 seconds. We might set an ideal or target as 30 seconds. Not every slide has to rotate at the exact same time interval.

Shorter than 20 seconds, and the streaming capability of the Internet gets clogged, so that your slides may not load quickly enough. Longer than one minute, and your participants may be bored looking at the same slide for that long.

Types of slides

The types of slides you can use match your imagination, and include clip art, photographs, charts, graphs, demonstrations, line drawing, cartoons, color mixes, screen shots from other web sites, and more.

Howles advises that the first few slides should be of simple construction, such as clip art, so that they can load quickly and stay with your audio presentation. If you have dense slides, such as photographs or rich artwork, intersperse them and separate them from each other with a couple of simple slides such as line drawings or clip art. The dense slides take more time to download, and separating them with some less complex slides keeps the streaming on time with less chance for interruption or clogging.

Storyboards

Storyboards help in thinking about your accompanying slide presentation, says Howles. A storyboard is created by taking sheets of paper and drawing a line down the middle. On the left side, you put your script, what you will say. On the right-hand side of the line, you put a description of your accompanying slides opposite the script copy when the slide will appear.

The Ability to Pause

The on-line audio/video, discussion groups have one common appeal to me: the ability to pause. I've always had trouble getting through a traditional lecture without some presented point sparking a chain of thoughts, and consequently a gap in my attention. Now I can pick up where I left off. The opportunity in discussion to stop and formulate a response encourages critical thinking in a way that F2F sometimes inhibits for those of us who are slow to find the right words.
— Lee Tarpley, Texas A&M Ag Research and Extension Center, Beaumont, TX

Who does your slide presentation

If you are able to do a PowerPoint presentation, then you should create the slides to accompany your audio lecture. It will take less time and be more what you want it to look like. If you are not proficient in doing PowerPoint presentations, don't worry. My approach is to spend my time and energy on the educational rather than technical aspects of teaching online, so I hire my teenage son, college students, high school students, and other low-cost but cheerful techies, often with some creative and artistic suggestions (at no additional cost), to help me. While you can ask your institution's technical or graphics support staff, waiting for or paying for a professional may exceed your time or expense budget. Low-cost help is bountiful.

Just do it

For your first online audio lecture, it is unlikely you will be able to incorporate all of the above tips and suggestions. Don't worry about it. Just do it. Just record your first online audio lecture. In subsequent audio lectures and revisions, you will begin to incorporate more of these recommendations. You will gain much from your own experience and from practicing the craft of creating online audio lectures. Enjoy the experience.

Podcasting

One day a faculty member in one of my online courses told everyone else that he had downloaded my audio lectures to his iPod and listened to them while walking in the woods. That anecdote illustrates that podcasting is a simple concept as it applies to online courses.

Podcasting your audio lectures simply means that your students download your audio lectures to a portable device like an iPod and listen wherever they want. If you have audio lectures posted, just check with your techie and ask whether your students can download them. If they can, you don't have to do anything.

For news programs and other newly created podcast programs, there is also something called RSS feeds. RSS stands for Really Simple Syndication. The RSS feed option gives students the additional ability to have your new weekly lectures automatically downloaded to their computer. As you probably have them all recorded already, the RSS feed option is likely neither necessary nor desireable. Consult your institution's techie and others about the necessity of RSS feeds.

Students Post Audio

It happened in my online class one day. A faculty participant from the University of Wisconsin-Madison recorded a two-minute message specific to our class and posted it in the class discussion area. I was pleasantly surprised. When I asked our techie, he said our server has been set to allow participants to post audio.

This is another great learning tool. With a $10 microphone, your students can record and post their verbal presentations, comments and other ideas in audio form in your online classroom. The more variety, the better. The more involvement from your students, the better. Students posting audio is another good technique to enhance their learning.

— Greg Brecht

Chapter 12
Creating Online Interaction

The heart and soul of your online course is not content, but interaction. This is where real learning and education takes place. It is the interplay between participants and you as teacher. And it is the interaction among the participants themselves.

Palloff and Pratt state unequivocally, "In the online classroom, it is the relationships and interactions among people through which knowledge is primarily generated. Key to the learning process are the interactions among students themselves, the interactions between faculty and students, and the collaboration in learning that results from these interactions.

"It is where your course comes alive. It is where your learners get excited, the adrenaline starts to flow, eyes widen, brain cells explode with new information, lights go on, fun happens."

"Online discussion areas offer many advantages you won't find in face-to-face settings," state Collison, et al, in *Facilitating Online Discussion*.

Only in an online course can you have people living in all corners of the globe participating at the same time. Only in an online course can you have everyone in the course talking at the same time. Only in an online course can you have so many participants you can divide up into small discussion groups based on special interest groups. This is what makes learning online so incredible.

This is also what distinguishes education from training. Training is generally a one-way street, with content delivered by an instructor, and absorbed by the participant. Education is more a two-way street, with the learners contributing ideas and experience, learning from each other, and sharing.

Time of Day

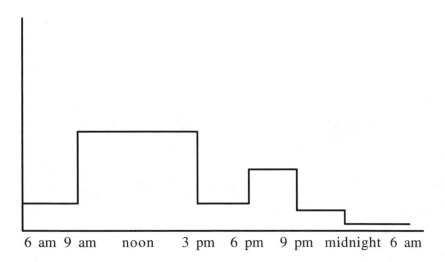

6 am 9 am   noon   3 pm   6 pm   9 pm   midnight 6 am

Sometimes there is a pattern to the hour of the day when other students and your instructor make comments online. Your course pattern may differ from this illustration.

Asynchronous Threaded Discussion

An asynchronous discussion forum, often called a threaded bulletin board, allows you and your students to make written comments online for everyone else in the class to see. The comments can be made any time day or night. They remain readable unless you decide to delete or archive them.

This will be your central meeting place on the Internet. This is where your participants will come to hear what you have to say, read your latest comments, ask questions, and have a group discussion.

This software feature is built into most if not all online classroom software. All you need to do is to use it.

Here you want to have an ongoing plan for interaction with your participants. Here are some tips and techniques in developing your inter-action plan for your online course:

1. Organize the main discussion area by unit. Every unit in your online course should have a corresponding online discussion about that unit's topic.

How long the discussion should last for each unit is dependent on how long the course lasts. If you have a one-week online course, then each discussion might be for one day. If you have a ten- to sixteen-week online course, then each discussion might last for a week. For sure the discussion should be open around the clock, 24 hours a day. This does not mean you have to sit in front of your computer all day. But it does allow your participants to make comments any time they wish.

2. Create a discussion topic or theme. Online teachers have found that the most successful way to generate online discussion each week is to outline or suggest a topic or theme.

You as teacher begin each unit's discussion to get it going, as well as demonstrate your ongoing involvement in the discussion. Some instructors create an initial question. Often, the initial question is meant to get the discussion started. At other times the instructor makes it mandatory for the student to respond in some way to the question.

3. Prepare for your online discussions. They won't just happen. There will not be a spontaneous outpouring of great insightful comments and questions from your participants. Initially, there will be 'dead air' as they say in the broadcasting business. So you will want to create the discussion, get it started, and give it momentum.

Here are a few tips related to planning your online discussion.
- Do 1-4 comments at the beginning of each unit discussion. Prepare them in advance.
- Try to line up participants or guest commentators to make initial comments or questions early on in the discussion to get the ball rolling.
- Inform your participants of the upcoming discussion with an e-mail. A daily e-mail to them is a great idea.

4. Secondary discussion areas. A number of online instructors have a secondary discussion area. Some instructors have a discussion area for non-course chat among students, like a student union or water cooler area. Others have an "Open Discussion" area for those topics that do not fit neatly into the main unit discussion. Still others have small group discussions, where students are divided up into small groups for online discussion. And of course a number of instructors simply have one area for discussion.

Open Ended

Post an open-ended question that asks students to describe the online class experience. I ask them to suggest a metaphor or offer a one-word description and then expand for 1-2 paragraphs. I allow anonymous posts for this discussion and I get some really interesting answers! It allows the students to debrief and vent some of their feelings. — Sue Stewart, University of Illinois, Champaign, IL

But after you have taught online for awhile, you may very well see the advantage in having a second asynchronous discussion forum.

On our site, we use the second discussion forum for "learners only." The instructors stay out of it, except to ask questions at the beginning of each day. This gives the class participants an opportunity to say anything they want, ask anything, or respond to other participants without having the presence of the all-knowing, authoritative, and sometimes intimidating instructor there to correct or comment.

5. Saving and archiving the discussions. One very positive and useful aspect of the asynchronous discussion forum is the ability to save and archive the discussion. By saving and archiving the discussion, your

participants can view and download the comments at any time in the future, as long as you want them to have access to it.

Other Uses of Threaded Bulletin Boards

Threaded bulletin boards are wonderful tools with many uses. In addition to using your threaded bulletin board for online discussion, you can create additional areas for other uses. Your online classroom software may already have some of these functions built in.

Here are some things you can do with threaded bulletin boards:

1. Message or comment board. If you want your participants to make comments on a number of different topics, a threaded bulletin board is a good way to go. Each thread would be a different topic, and your participants would post their comments on the appropriate thread.

2. An individual record. If you want each of your participants to post information, homework, or comments, you could set up a threaded bulletin board. Each thread would be the name of a different person in your class, and the person would post her or his comments in his or her own thread.

3. Daily question. Every day, you could ask a different question and have all your participants respond. Each thread would then be a separate date, along with the question of the day.

4. Directories, references, and much more. There are many other uses for threaded bulletin boards. They are used as directories of individuals. They are used to store references to other information, books and links. They are used as an online "classified ads" section, with people buying and selling products or just posting ideas. Use a threaded bulletin board if it is useful for you.

Real-Time Chat Rooms

A real-time chat room, sometimes called an IRC (Internet Relay Chat), is a synchronous chat room, which means the discussion takes place at a given time.

First-time online teachers and students often think of online interaction as taking place in real time. However, the vast majority of online teachers use the asynchronous threaded bulletin board for discussion.

We don't know how to talk online yet

Some online instructors use real-time chat occasionally as a secondary means for dialogue or just to maintain communication with the class. Many online education authorities, such as Palloff and Pratt, do not recommend using the real-time chat room at all. Venture into real-time online chat at your own risk. If you want to use this device, you set up a time of the day for a chat and invite or encourage all your participants to get online at the same time.

There are two challenges with real-time chat rooms for online classes:

A. *Time differences.* If your participants are all in the same time zone, then there is no problem. But more and more online courses will want and benefit from having participants in many different time zones, and thus scheduling a time when everyone is awake, much less available, becomes difficult.

B. *Short comments.* A real-time chat room only has the capability for short comments. Longer comments do not work well on a real-time chat room because of the time it takes to post them, and because comments scroll up and out of view so very quickly.

Real-time chat rooms may have a place in your online course. But again, there is the problem of trying to get everyone on at the same time, possibly dealing with different time zones.

Some online instructors use real-time chat for office hours, so that students can communicate with them in real time about any issue.

E-mail

E-mail is a wonderful tool and has many uses. Use e-mail to:

- Contact everyone in the course at various times, update them on changes in the course, or simply encourage them to participate online.
- For strictly individual to individual comments, including dealing with a learner's problems, e-mail is the only way to go.
- Use e-mail autoresponders to send information to prospective participants for an upcoming course.
- E-mail test scores or evaluative comments to your participants.

E-mail should NOT be used as the central discussion or dialogue mode of communication. E-mail does not allow others to participate or benefit from learner questions, comments and sharing. And communicating with your students via e-mail is very time consuming. But for many other communication issues, e-mail is a great tool.

Preparing Your Online Discussion

Online discussion won't just happen. You will want to prepare for your online discussion. Here are some items to plan in advance:

Number and types of discussion areas.
For classes with a small number of participants (fewer than 30) you may want to have only 1-2 discussion areas. For larger classes (more than 30), you might want 2-3 discussion areas. You get to decide.

> ## Online assignments
> Specific assignments are needed for basic learning in the course, but my best discussion lie in creating assignments that are not very specific in how to do something. These assignments have very specific goals established for students. But by creating a discussion revolving around the path that needs to occur to get to that goal, students learn more about my subject. I mix specific and non-specific assignments to give a deeper knowledge and exercise critical thinking. I have found that this also results in very good discussions as students truly explore the material. — Kevin Lewis, University of Wyoming, Laramie, WY

Almost every online course has a discussion area for teacher-student dialogue, where you communicate with your students, and where they dialogue with you as facilitator.

A number of online instructors have found additional discussion areas useful. Some types of discussion areas include:

- *Student-only discussion.* In this threaded discussion, you as teacher do not make comments. Only your students make comments.
- *Virtual water cooler.* In this area, your students can chit-chat about things other than your course.
- *Small group discussions.* For classes of 10 or more students, a number of instructors divide the class up into small groups, each with their own discussion area.
- *Special interest groups.* You can create optional special interest groups, where students with a particular specialty interest can pursue the topic more in-depth than the rest of the class might.
- *Guest speakers or experts.* Guest commentators or experts might

dialogue with your class in your main discussion area, but you might also set up a separate area for their comments and interactions.

- *Exercises or projects.* If your course involves certain exercises or projects, you could establish a separate threaded bulletin board for students to work or report on their projects.

Rules for discussion areas.

For each different discussion area, you should create certain rules or guidelines. The guidelines should include who posts there and what kinds of comments or postings are made.

Number of comments.

Most instructors let their students know that they expect a minimum number of online comments in a given time period, which is usually a week. And instructors teaching for credit often require a minimum number of comments per week, which is a sound educational practice online. Few if any online instructors set a maximum number of comments, and many online learning experts view online discussion as "the more, the better."

The minimum number of comments per week per student that online instructors expect or require ranges from one to three. Some instructors encourage 2-3, but accept one as the minimum.

Discussion questions and starter comments.

For each module or unit, you will want to create some discussion questions or starter comments to get the discussion going. The type of question or comment you initially make at the start of each unit or week significantly influences the direction the discussion takes, and also the level of discussion.

So spend some time in advance of your course planning what discussion questions you will ask for each unit to create the kind of online dialogue you want from your course.

Orient your students.

In your orientation for your students, you will want to make some remarks about the importance and value of the online discussion in your course, as well as make some preliminary comments about how you and they can create a "safe" online learning environment so everyone can share their ideas.

In your orientation, tell them:

- *Your expectations.* Let them know exactly what you want to have happen, including how many times they should make a comment during each unit.

- *What to do.* Tell them what to do, including the characteristics of a good comment or posting.
- *How to read and write comments.* Give them some technical pointers, such as how to use "Find in page" on their browser. Tell them the different ways to read comments (for example, by chronology, or by thread, or by participant). Give them some tips on how to write a comment, such as HTML language to create a link within a message. This can be just one paragraph of information. Make it positive, enthusiastic, and encouraging.

Points per Unit

I have 3 points per unit for completing the learning activity (case scenario analysis, discussion questions, etc.) And two points per unit for responding a minimum of once per each thread. I tell the students to go through the postings, find an "ah ha" and respond to it with their own experiences or knowledge or with a thoughtful question. — Veronica Taylor, University of Wyoming, Laramie, WY

Some questions teachers ask about creating online interaction

Q1. Can I get to know my students online?

A1. Yes. Here's what online teaching authority Dr. Rita-Marie Conrad says, "I love being in cyberspace and my learners love being in cyberspace. We share a lot of things. I get to know them, their joys and tragedies and about their families. We are a family in an online community."

Q2. Aren't written comments impersonal and anonymous?

A2. No, online interaction is very personal.

Q3. What about shy people online?

A3. Often people who are shy in face-to-face interactions are more apt to be able to speak out online and express themselves.

Q4. How can I facilitate a discussion when I can't see body movement and facial expressions?

A4. You will discover other cues in your students' comments. You will be able to detect a student's level of confidence, interest level, depth of reflection and other individual learning behaviors in his or her comments, which are very revealing.

Q5. Can you teach critical thinking online?

A5. Yes. Collison, et al, in *Facilitating Online Learning* have an excellent section on questions you can ask to stimulate critical thinking, which they adapted from Dennis Mathies's work on critical thinking called *Precision Questioning* (1991).

Wiki Technology

Online communication expert Debbie Weil notes that one of the big new trends likely to become a part of 21st century culture is that "customers create content." For you, your customers are your students.

Having your students create content is another online technique to both engage your students and enhance their learning. Wiki technology is one tool in which you can do that. Wiki pages are web pages in which anyone can change the words. Words can be deleted, changed, added, and so forth. At the time of this edition, Wikipedia was the best known wiki web site.

Wiki pages is just another option in your online teaching tool kit. If you are interested, ask your techie how to create wiki pages.

Blogs

Weblogs, or blogs for short, is a popular way to communicate your thoughts for a simple but very good reason: blog creators have made it so easy to use, and so attractive for your readers to view.

When you subscribe (currently fairly inexpensive) to a blog creator, you get your own blog to do with what you wish.

The most popular format for blogs is to use it as a diary, journal or other personal entry, with the added feature that your readers can then make comments in response to your postings. Other features make blogs attractive, like the addition of pictures, links to other web sites, and the ability to write them in advance and schedule the day and time of posting.

Blogs at this time are an optional tool to consider. If you do, think about getting a little creative with your blog. For example, think about:

- Multi-class blog. Do one blog for several classes.
- Collaborate with other professors. Do one blog in conjunction with other professors and classes.

- <u>Partner with other colleges, or countries</u>. Partner with instructors in other colleges who are teaching the same subject matter. Think about whether a teacher or college in another country would add an interesting perspective for your students.
- <u>Ask professionals</u>. Ask professionals to be guest-bloggers and submit some columns for your blog, giving your students other views and experiences.

Chapter 13
Designing Online Assessment

The third major component of an online course is assessment. Assessments are most often thought of as tests and quizzes, but on the Internet the whole nature of tests and quizzes changes, enhancing learning and contributing positively to the learning experience. Doing assessments is not necessary for an online course, but it is such a valuable tool for learners, so easy to implement, and full of so much potential that doing assessments for your online course will be a great addition to your teaching.

Before we discuss ways to design and implement assessments, we need to talk a little about how outcomes, measurements, and evaluations of learning experiences will change in the Information Age and online.

In the Industrial Age, the 20th century, a major part of assessment was based on attendance, just being there. As Woody Allen is purported to have said, "90% of success is just showing up." Many measurements of education are based on attendance. For example, take continuing education units, or CEUs, one measurement of continuing education for adults. A CEU is earned by attending an educational program of ten hours.

But online, attendance is both difficult to measure, and irrelevant. It is not difficult to measure the number of times a person logs on to your course. But what the person is doing while logging on is much harder to determine.

New technologies may solve the problem of measuring participation, but the bigger issue is that attendance, or putting in one's time, is now irrelevant. What matters now is outcomes and results — whether you or I have actually learned something. It matters much less how much time we put into the effort. You may learn Unit 1 in half the time I do, and I may learn Unit 2 in half the time you do. Every person putting the same amount of time into the same subject matter, regardless of

---

How To Teach Adults

Please enter your Name: [   ] *(required)*

Quiz	Remaining Attempts
⦿ Day 1	*Unlimited*
○ Day 2	*Unlimited*
○ Day 3	*Unlimited*
○ Day 4	*Unlimited*
○ Day 5 - Final	*Unlimited*

[Take a Quiz]

Quiz:Day 1

1. **Which of the following is NOT an important characteristic of adult learners and adult learning:**

   a. ○ Family characteristics
   b. ○ Emotional characteristics
   c. ○ Physical characteristics
   d. ○ Mental characteristics
   e. ○ Social characteristics

2. **The key to A learner's positive emotional climate is:**

   a. ○ Motivation
   b. ○ Discipline
   c. ○ Self-image
   d. ○ Level of formal schooling

3. **Which of the following is NOT A characteristic of adult learners:**

   a. ○ Readiness to learn
   b. ○ Future orientation
   c. ○ Problem orientation
   d. ○ Time perspective

4. **The most important social characteristic of adult learners is an abundance and variety of:**

   a. ○ Backgrounds
   b. ○ Stories
   c. ○ Jokes
   d. ○ Experiences

Example of a multiple-choice online quiz. After completing, results can be instantly analyzed and returned to you.

previous experience, aptitude for that subject, or ability to learn, no longer makes sense.

And so we are moving towards outcomes and results as a measure of learning. If you pass the test, you know the stuff. It doesn't matter how much time you put in, or how many times you logged on, if you pass it, you know it. And if you don't pass the test, you don't know it.

This change in desired outcomes in learning from attendance to results is causing a change in the way we do tests and evaluations as well. We are moving towards more core questions, more questions dealing with the central ideas and skills of the course.

What this means is that online, both teacher and learner can reap enormous benefits from the new possibilities of doing assessments. Here are three different kinds of assessments to consider for your online course.

Pre-Course Assessment

Use a pre-course assessment in two ways: First, to help prospect participants determine whether your online course is right for them; and second, to determine the level of knowledge of each of your participants before they begin your course.

Here's how to do it. Create a ten-question, multiple-choice quiz. Ten questions is enough to get a good sense of the knowledge of the person, but short enough that most people won't be deterred from taking the quiz. The questions should be ones that people will be able to answer at the end of your course. In fact, they could even be the questions from your final exam, assuming you have a final exam.

For prospective participants determining whether your online course is right for them, the pre-course assessment is helpful in several ways:

1. It tells them about the content of your course and what they will learn. The questions on your quiz will reflect what they can expect to learn. If this is not the subject matter they were hoping for, it is better for them, and you, that they not enroll. So this information is helpful to them.

2. It tells them how much they already know. If, for some reason, they know all the material already, then they may not need the course. This rarely happens. What usually happens is that people do poorly on the pre-course assessment, and the quiz helps show them how much they will learn by taking your course.

3. The quiz establishes a benchmark for both you as a teacher and the individual learner. By measuring how well a person does before

taking your course, you are now able to measure progress and demonstrate how much they gained from the course by comparing their pre-course score with their final evaluation score.

4. Another benefit is that you as instructor have a good idea what your participants know, and don't know, as they come to your course. This will help you emphasize certain content areas, spend less time on the things they already know, and in general help you teach them better.

The results of the pre-course assessment should be made available immediately to the person taking the quiz. The results should be stored so that you, as teacher, can have access to them to assist you in preparing your course and in benchmarking the person's pre- and post-course scores. No one else need know the quiz scores.

Discussion Points

For an online nursing chemistry course, points are required to be earned for discussion. Students are required to earn 80 online points by the end of the semester, but they can earn no more than 12 points every two weeks. Points are assigned for their discussion of topics or questions they have posted. Points are assigned based on the relevance and accuracy of their comments. Points are never subtracted, only added. The online points earned have correlated well with their test scores. — Vicky Bevilacqua, Kennesaw State University, Marietta, GA

Progress Assessments

A terrific new opportunity for learning now exists online in helping your participants measure their progress on a weekly or even daily basis. While it is possible that some teachers may have given weekly or daily tests using paper and pencil, it has not been common nor easy. Now it is so easy that progress assessments will be a great learning and teaching tool.

Once again, you devise a ten-question, multiple-choice quiz. Once again, it does not have to be exactly ten questions. You post the quizzes in your online classroom. There are several technical software programs to make this quite easy to do, and the major online classroom software providers have this feature built in already.

The correct answers are immediately given back to the participant, so she knows how well she has done. The person can then review some material she missed, or move ahead if the scores look pretty good. These self-quizzes are not part of hte student's grade.

You as an instructor then have the option of getting the progress assessment scores, or not. If they are helpful to you and if you have the time, you can review them and adjust your teaching. If you have a large number of participants in your online course, or more limited time, you don't have to review the scores.

If you are interested in monitoring the progress of each participant more closely, the progress assessment quizzes will help you do that. If a person scores low on a series of quizzes, then you and that person know there is some special effort that has to be made. If a person does not even take the quiz, then you know something as well.

Progress assessment quizzes are a great learning tool. They will speed up the learning. They will refocus the learning around the areas that need attention for a particular learner. And they will inform you as teacher how well folks are doing, and whether you need to be more advanced, back up, repeat some material, or move more quickly in your instruction.

Student Evaluations

The third use of an assessment is to evaluate your participants and how much a student has learned by the end of your course.

Some kinds of participant evaluations take place online. Other kinds of student evaluation can take place offline, in the manner of a traditional face-to-face classroom. If you are uncomfortable with online evaluations, then use traditional offline kinds of evaluations.

More experienced online instructors use multiple kinds of assessment instead of a single evaluation method such as a test. By designing a set of assessments, you as a teacher may get a better picture of how well an individual participant is doing in your course. We also know that, just as we each learn in different ways, different learners assess differently, some doing better on tests, others doing better with group projects, and so on.

Thus, we provide you with a list of options for student evaluations. All of the options provided below have been used by one or more online instructors. There do not appear to be certain kinds of evaluations that online learning experts deem better than others. Tests, online comments, papers and projects are probably more common in online courses than other kinds of evaluations.

The one theme or direction we can point to for participant evaluations in online courses is the use of multiple assessments, and this diversity in evaluation methods is enriching the practice of evaluations for both teachers and students.

Essays and papers

This traditional evaluation method is used fairly commonly in online courses. There are a few enhancements and variations to the essay or paper in online courses. Essays and papers can be e-mailed as attachments to you, or posted in the online classroom, which helps you coordinate and save time on paperwork. You can require a certain kind of format, such as Word, to make the analysis and grading easier. Some teachers require essays and papers to be submitted in a markable format, including Adobe, so that the instructor can easily make comments on a draft document and return it quickly to the student for further work.

Video Cam to Monitor Testing

Imagine in the future the use of computer cams to the monitoring location at each computer station to help confirm "no cheating." With Net Meeting and setting up a buddy list this is already possible with small groups. — Denise McWilliams, North Dakota State University, Fargo, ND

Online comments

Both the quality and quantity of individual student comments are commonly used as evaluation criteria in online courses. A standard requirement for online postings is one comment a week for each student. For credit courses, making online comments mandatory has been successful.

A number of experienced online instructors have developed point systems for online comments. For instance, Collison, et al, provide an illustration in which an isolated or unconnected comment is given .5 points, a response to another comment is given 1 point, and a response that integrates multiple views gets 2 points.

Timed online quizzes

Several online classrooms have a built-in feature for timed online quizzes. During a certain time period, any time a student logs on to your course, a short quiz (usually with 1-5 multiple-choice questions) will automatically pop up. The student will have a set amount of time to complete the quiz, such as five or ten minutes. The quiz results are then forwarded to the instructor.

Proctored tests or exams

A number of online course instructors use proctored tests or exams. The exam is mailed to a proctor, an individual located near the student, who administers the exam and verifies that the student alone took the exam, there were no outside materials available, no other person was present, and the time of starting and ending. Instead of an individual proctor, some instructors have used commercial testing centers to administer exams.

Individual projects

Some individual projects are all online, where a student engages in an online project using the web and the results are posted online. Other individual projects are offline and involve traditional project methods.

Group projects

With the need for collaboration in the workplace growing, we may see more group projects in online courses as they help students prepare to work collaboratively. We already know that younger students often learn better collaboratively, which provides another rationale for using group projects as an evaluation tool.

Online group projects provide the least problems logistically. Offline group projects in which people need to get together face-to-face may pose some problems for some students.

Group project evaluations may involve assessing how the group functioned as well as the project outcome. And there is also the issue of assessing individuals within a group who may have performed above or below the level of the group as a whole.

Online tests and quizzes

Your online classroom software will have a test or quiz capability built-in. There are options for true-false, multiple choice, matching, fill in the blank, and short answer questions. Some software have a feature where you can post pictures, drawings or other visuals as part of the question (for example, name the planet in the picture). They may have a feature for online essay questions. A computer can instantly grade online tests and quizzes, with the exception of essay questions. Be careful about short answer and fill-in-the-blank answer grading as well. Online tests can be given for each unit, and/or as a final test.

Mentored practice

Mentored practice has been used in certain classes in which skills, such as clinical skills, are involved. The instructor finds an experienced practitioner in the geographical location of the student and this "mentor" then assists the student in developing and practicing the set of skills. The mentor then evaluates the student or confirms that the skill level has been achieved.

Edit Papers with Adobe

Some of the online instructors at my university are going to require the use of Adobe Acrobat for papers for two reasons, (1) inability to access written work that has been completed by a word processor different from the one you are using and (2) you can make corrections/modifications in participants' papers using Adobe... much like was described in Microsoft. In addition Adobe keeps the "format" the same as the original paper whereas this may not always happen in other word processing programs. — Amy Finch, Fort Hays State University, Hays, KS

Rita-Marie Conrad offers these additional options for evaluation:

Individual presentations

An online presentation could be done in text, leading an online discussion, responding to questions in an online discussion, as a specially constructed home page or web site, as an audio file the student records and e-mails to you, or as a videocam report, either live or recorded.

Group presentations

Group presentations have mostly been accomplished with text or online discussions. Guidelines could be established to present a "panel" of comments, responses, or debate in your threaded discussion area.

Analysis of case studies

Students take one or more case studies and do their own analysis of the case study, providing not only suggested outcomes or resolutions in the studies but also documenting their resources and how they arrived at those conclusions.

Reflective journals

A more personal, sometimes chronological, analysis, often involving the learner's own growth and development, attitudes and beliefs, or changes in behavior.

Debates

You establish the rules, how points are scored, the subject, and the teams. Be sure to give the debate enough time (between 3-7 days might be an appropriate range) so all participants have a chance to be fully involved.

Role plays

One kind of online role play involves you providing a hypothetical scenario and assigning different roles to each of your students (for example, the stressed out housewife; the truant teenager, etc.). Another kind of online role play involves an historical era in which each of your students becomes an historical figure (for example, Napoleon, Josephine, the Russian general, the English general, the Pope, etc.).

Tests as Games

An excellent technique is to turn your self-assessments from tests into games, says online learning expert William Horton.

Horton says that the number of participants who take the knowledge tests will increase if they are created as games rather than tests, and that the anxiety level of the students will decrease as well. Game formats for quizzes include the "Jeopardy" format, the "Who Wants to Be a Millionaire" format, crossword puzzles, and drag and click placement of certain objects. Horton recommends different difficulty levels, just like in games, for positive reinforcement and support.

Cheating Online

Another one of the most popular questions about online teaching is how to tell if the person taking an online test is really the person who registered for the course. If you are concerned about cheating online, use traditional offline evaluations. A number of instructors use this strategy.

A few quick observations about online cheating:

- Although online cheating is a hot topic among teachers, there are few reported instances of online cheating.
- Online cheating is seemingly no easier than cheating in a traditional course.
- Technology will soon provide an efficient, if somewhat frightening in its privacy implications, solution to identifying computer users online.
- Do not create a trust issue between yourself and the vast majority of students who will participate in your course honestly and with full integrity.

The best response to a concern about cheating online is to build in a variety of evaluation measurements and activities into your online course that also are positive learning tools and experiences.

It is also recommended you not spend too much time and energy on this issue until it becomes a problem.

Learner Questionnaire

Prepare learners ahead of time with a questionnaire. Before the class starts, prepare learners ahead of time by sending them a questionnaire and get them thinking and planning about their online course.

Solutions

Here are several things you can do to reduce the risk of online cheating in your course:

- *Require online comments.* By requiring online comments on a weekly basis, you substantially make it more difficult and more expensive for a student to cheat.
- *Require unit quizzes.* Unit quizzes make it more expensive for a student to cheat, and if the student takes some quizzes and an imposter takes a final exam, the statistical discrepancy in scores is readily identified.
- *Do spontaneous quizzes.* Use the timed quiz feature in your online classroom software. There is less likelihood of a student contacting an imposter and getting answers within a five minute test period.
- *Make a phone call.* Call a suspect student and simply ask him or her a question or two that they got correct on a recent test.
- *Compare papers.* Several web sites provide software and techniques to detect plagiarism in papers.

To reiterate, the best strategy is use a variety of evaluation methods, including unit quizzes, online comments, and projects. The variety and regularity of the testing reduces the chances of cheating, raises the cost of cheating, and most importantly, constitute positive learning activities for the vast majority of your participants who are honest and participate with integrity in your course. And if you are still concerned about cheating online, use traditional offline evaluations.

Use Grading Rubric

For those topics that are subjective you might want to research the use of a MI/Lfu Creative Grading Rubric and assessment (see page 95 of *Coloring Outside the Lines* by Rene Diaz-Lefebvre, Ph.D.). I personally plan to incorporate the same type of testing and research writing that would be done in a traditional class. The only major change would come in the form of a participation grade and the delivery of material.
— Dennis Morgan, Lima Technical College, Lima, OH

Cheating is harder online

There are several reasons why cheating online is probably harder than cheating in a traditional classroom setting. In a traditional course, an imposter usually has to be engaged only once, either to write a paper or take an exam. Online, an imposter has to be engaged regularly, for unit quizzes, online comments, projects, papers and final exams. The repeated need for an imposter means the cost of hiring someone to cheat goes up. Finally, in an online environment, the work of the student and that of an imposter can be compared much more easily, so that differences, discrepancies and patterns of word usage can be compared much more easily.

The technology solution

The solution long-term to online cheating is technology. And "long-term" in technology terms could be any day now.

Companies have been reported to be working on several identification techniques. One is retinal identification, in which the computer, and thus you as instructor, can identify the user from the user's unique eye patterns. In a recent radio news interview, a businessman spoke about being able to identify fingerprints using the mouse pad. Another security expert indicated that there are individual patterns of typing on a keyboard which can identify a user. And a growing use of videocams by computer users is another identification possibility.

Most of these solutions are being developed not for educational use, but for corporate and work environment monitoring. For many educators, the technological solutions to online cheating may pose greater concerns about privacy, monitoring, and working relationships in the online environment.

The risk factor

Not many people are willing to risk embarrassment, much less their career and good name, for the sake of cheating in an online course. People have been cheating in courses for centuries, and will continue to do so without impacting the validity or reputation of the course, teacher or sponsoring organization. Don't spend too much time worrying about this issue.

Multiple Assessments

If we learn differently, do we also test differently? The answer is yes. Your students differ in their ability to demonstrate learning and knowledge based on the type of assessment being given.

Thus one of the forward thinking advances that online instructors are making is to create multiple assessments for grading purposes. Grades in online classes often consist of four or more different kinds of assessments.

Using a number of different assessments allows students to better demonstrate their knowledge and learning, as one measurement in learning does not fit all students. The four most common assessments in online courses appear to be tests, essays or other written assignment, online discussion, and projects. You should be as creative as you need to be in developing your own mix of assessments.

Eventually, there will be an individual contract between the student and teacher on how the student will be evaluated. The evaluation will be based on the student's strengths, not weaknesses. The goal of assessment in this century is to assess what a student knows or has learned. Multiple assessments are a great advancement that can be primarily credited to online instructors.

Gender Bias in Grading

Males and females learn differently (Gurian, 2001). In some cases, genders may perform differently on certain kinds of assessments.

Overall, males and females perform the same on tests, according to the College Board, Educational Testing Service, and other testing authorities. So cumulatively males and females learn the same amount and gain the same level of knowledge. However, females perform much better in general with verbal and language skills. Males perform better with spatial skills (Willingham and Cole, 1997).

In grading your online students, look at the cumulative scores for all your classes by gender to see if males or females do better on any of your assessments. If so, consider giving students an alternative assessment measure.

Alternative Assessment Measures

Consider using an alternative assessment measure when needed. Students with learning differences (sometimes labeled disabilities), different native language or culture, gender, or even age may require an alternative assessment measure to accurately measure their learning.

Here's an example of an alternative assessment measure. Willie's class had to read a book. To determine whether each student had read the book, the instructor gave a short quiz. Willie couldn't answer any of the questions. Instead of giving him a failing score, the instructor engaged Willie in a verbal conversation. In the conversation, Willie explained why he thought there was no one hero in the book (one of the questions), but many possible candidates, and in several other ways demonstrated that he indeed had read the book. By using an alternative measure, the teacher was able to make a more fair assessment, and respond to the individual learning (and assessment) differences of his students.

Engaging Students in Evaluation

Your students benefit when they participate in the evaluation of themselves and other students, say Rita-Marie Conrad and J. Ana Donaldson (Conrad & Donaldson, 2004, page 27). Students can be engaged in the assessment of:

- Online discussion. "In an engaged learning environment, peers often have the best perspective on whether their teammates are providing valuable contributions to the learning community," write Conrad and Donaldson.
- Projects. "By including team assessments as part of the project

grade, the instructor can emphasize the importance of collaboration," say Conrad and Donaldson.

- Self-assessments. "Reflection and self-assessment are important components for empowerment in any learner-focused environment," note Conrad and Donaldson.

More and more faculty are engaging students in assessment activities, changing the way evaluations are being conducted. Engaging students in the process helps them analyze their own learning achievements, is a learning process in and of itself, contributes to collaboration, may give you as instructor a different perspective or new information, and can help restructure instructor time to focus more on assisting your learners.

Post Grades Online

Be sure to post project, test, assignment and other scores online in the student's own secure web area. Companies providing online grading systems report that student grades go up 8% on average when scores are posted online, simply because students know where they stand at any given point and can adjust their studying accordingly.

Post Assignments Online

While it may be a given that assignments in an online course are posted online, there are two important things that need to be said. First, understand that in the 21st century, verbal and handwritten instructions are simply too imprecise, too subjective, and too susceptible to misinterpretation. Online instructions are a must for students (and workers) to ensure precision and mutual understanding. Second, make your assignment instructions as detailed as possible. Leave no assumption unaddressed, state or restate everything for maximum clarity.

Generation Y, and succeeding generations in this century, require detailed instructions that are understood and documented. Posting assignments online represents a significant and positive shift in communication for the learning and work places.

The Future of Assessment

Evaluation of student learning is in the beginning stages of an enormous transition from the factory model of the last century to a personalisation (sic) model relevant for this century.

Here are some of the key aspects of that transition:

Personalisation.

Professor Diana Laurillard, a leading educator in the United Kingdom, has stated, and an official UK education department planning document has endorsed, the concept of "personalisation" of learning, and therefore assessment (Laurillard, 2006).

This is really the long term direction and goal of all education in this century, to assist each student as an individual to reach his or her maximum potential. To that end, evaluation must be individualized in order to accurately and fairly what each student has learned and achieved academically.

Behavior irrelevant.

Much grading of students, quite frankly, is based on "behavior unrelated to learning and knowledge" (Coates and Draves, 2006). According to Educational Testing Service researchers (Willingham and Cole, 1997) only 47% of females and just 44% of males receive grades roughly equivalent to their test scores. That means that over half of students today receive grades that do not match their learning and knowledge achievement. We have to start grading students based on what they know and have learned, instead of their behavior.

From Time Input to Outcomes

In the last century, we measured performance largely by the amount of time that was input (Draves and Coates, Nine Shift, 2004). People were paid based on hours worked, not outcomes delivered. Students to a large measure are still judged based on time input. Most schools and colleges do not even have measures of learning outcomes and knowledge performance that allow students to learn at their own rates of speed. In the most antiquated of educational situations, students who take twice as long to learn a given amount of material are given more credit or better scores than students who learn the same amount of material in half the time.

The days of measuring learning by time input are limited. The real world of the 21st century is interested in performance and outcomes.

Start with Assessment

Kevin Lewis of the University of Wyoming begins with assessment in building his online courses, and recommends that other professors do so as well. By starting with assessment, one starts with the knowledge and learning outcomes desired. Curriculum, content, and discussion then are formulated around what you want your students to know at the end of the course. Evaluation should not be an afterthought, or last thought, but the place to begin.

In some sense, the drive for new types of assessment, new requirements for evaluation, and new ways of assessing learning and knowledge is helping to change the entire way we build and teach courses, both online and face-to-face. You are encouraged to join the challenge and excitement of creating new and better ways of assessment.

Part IV.
Teaching Your
Online Course

Chapter 14
Establishing the
Learning Environment

Establishing a positive online learning environment is one of the most important things you do as a teacher to help your participants learn online. This process starts when you are developing your online course, and includes how you create your online classroom, construct your agenda, welcome your participants, and initiate online conversation in the first critical week. By creating a learning community you enhance the learning of all your participants.

Constructing an Agenda

A week or so before the beginning of your course, your participants should have an agenda. The agenda should tell them:
- *What technical requirements* or software they need in order to participate in your course.
- *The course goals and objectives.*
- *An outline of the content* — topics or modules — included in your course. After each topic, you will want to include the readings, audio, links, and other content available pertaining to that topic or module.
- *The schedule* for interaction, dialogue, discussion forums, or chats.
- *The pre-assessment quiz*, or instructions on completing it, if you have one.
- *Rules or guidelines for participating* in the course. This might include:

- Expectations, such as the number of times a person should get online, or noting that participants are expected to make comments during the discussions or chats.
- Procedures, such as how and when to e-mail the instructor, the format in which a paper should be submitted, or how and when to communicate with other participants.
- Ethics, such as using your real name rather than a made up name online, not presenting others' work as your own, or not getting help or assistance on the tests.

Team Meeting

I have my students meet face-to-face before the online class starts. We form teams of 4-5 people, and each team is responsible for selecting questions from the readings to submit to the teacher, as well as a course project.

The teams have jelled so quickly and so well, I am convinced that part of it was the face-to-face meeting at the beginning. — Allan E. Pevoto, PhD, St. Edwards University, Austin, TX

- *Participants list.* The list can be basic, including name, address and so on. Or you could enhance the participants list in a variety of ways to encourage people to get to know one another and interact in and outside of your online course. You could:
  - Provide e-mail addresses, so participants can communicate with each other.
  - Have a short biography. Participants could write one paragraph, which you post on your site, about themselves. It could be biographical, or it could be about their interests and experiences in the subject matter of your course.
  - Picture. Participants post pictures of themselves, or have a link to other sites where their pictures are posted.
  - Web site link. Many people have their own web site, or are part of organizations with web sites, and you could provide the URL to your participants' web sites.
- *Where to go and pre-course activities.* You should tell participants how to get into your online course. And you might want to have them test your site out a day or two before the course starts to make sure they are comfortable with navigating your site.
- *Problems or questions.* Always have some address, place, or person

to contact in case a participant has a problem or question. It could be your e-mail address. It could be your webmaster's e-mail or phone number. It could be a toll-free phone number. Reassure your participants by giving them a contact in case they encounter a problem or question.

The agenda, along with a nice welcome from you as instructor, should be sent to participants. It could go out at the time they register for your course. It could be sent a week before. You could mail it, or e-mail it.

Creating a Learning Community

Dr. Rita-Marie Conrad notes, "We no longer deliver courses. Instead, we create 'knowledge environments'." Palloff & Pratt, in *Building Learning Communities in Cyberspace*, also see the "learning community" as a central concept, goal and practice in the online classroom. Hagel and Armstrong call it a "virtual community," and indicate that we may want to help create learning communities whose lives extend beyond the length of our courses, assisting in the mission of lifelong learning.

While you plan your learning community in the development of your online course, the creation of the learning community takes place from the student's first contact with the course at registration to about the second week of the course. So from about two weeks before your class starts to about two weeks after the course has begun is when you build the foundations your learning community.

Boettcher and Conrad suggest several class activities to build a learning community, including:

- Student introductions, spending some time the first week having each student introduce her- or himself online.
- Pre-interaction, such as introductory exercises or getting to know the technology.
- Interactive activities, such as online projects or other activities in which two or more participants work together.
- Collaborative activities, such as small group discussions.
- Cooperative activities, such as role plays and team projects.

Another community building technique is to have a threaded discussion area for students to chat about things other than the course. Many online teachers use this technique. Palloff & Pratt offer several different titles for this cyberspace water cooler area, such as Cyberspace Sandbox, the Coffee House, the Lounge, and Important Stuff.

Student Orientation

Every institution reports that retention has improved, with fewer student drop outs and greater achievement and satisfaction, as student orientation has increased. That is, the solution to online retention and satisfaction is to have more student orientation.

Student Orientation consists of two parts: technical orientation; and learning orientation. Don't forget to include how we learn online and the learning aspect of an online course in your Student Orientation.

Generally, the requirement is to pass the Student Orientation test; with the other meetings voluntary, optional or alternative benefits.

What works. It all works. Practitioners have reported success with all of these techniques, including:

- Week-long student orientation.
- Face-to-face student orientation for online classes, in addition to online orientation.
- Quizzes for students to take to "pass" orientation, or for their own benefit.
- Real-time chats as one option and opportunity.
- Requiring completion of online orientation before receiving password to the course.
- Student mentors or peer tutors.

Welcoming Your Participants

Your greeting may only be two or three sentences. It may only take three minutes. But it is very important that you welcome your participants. Tell them you are glad they are participating. Reinforce that they will get something valuable out of the course. Express your pleasure at the quantity or quality of the participants who are involved. Convey your excitement about them contributing to the course. Reassure them. It is very important you set the stage before you begin your course. As Jerry Apps once said, "Make them believe."

A few ways to break the ice online:

- On the first minute of the first hour of the course, type in your discussion forum or chat room a short one paragraph comment welcoming people to your course.
- Invite all participants to simply type their name and indicate they are logged on that day.
- Invite all participants to make a short statement about who they

are, why they came, or their previous experience in the subject area. Make it an easy task, something people do not have to think too much about, and something that tells a little something about each one as a person.
- Tell people if they are having problems or questions, to contact you immediately.

However you do it, welcome people to your course. It will put them in a positive frame of mind about their involvement in your course.

Muddiest Point

I created a "Muddiest Point" discussion board where students can post questions about the week's readings. At first, the students didn't seem to think it was helpful. As the semester progressed, they were checking in often. It seemed to offer confirmation that they weren't the only ones struggling with a concept or idea and made them feel less isolated. — Sue Stewart, University of Illinois, Champaign, IL

The First Day

The first day of your online course is the most important day of the course, regardless of how long your online course will be. If the first day goes well, you are off to a good start. If the first day goes poorly, you have damage control to do, and some courses never fully recover from a bad first day. If something goes wrong on the fifth week, they will forgive you. But if something goes wrong on the first day, their enthusiasm will be dimmed, they will expect further things to go wrong, and they will begin to question whether they made a good choice.

Here are some things to think about to make your first day online go well:
- **Technical back-up.** The Internet goes down. Wires get overloaded. Computers get glitches. Things happen. Do whatever you can do to ensure that things go technically well the first day. You should be at a computer with good connections. Try not to be traveling, on the road or working from a hotel on the first day. See if you can get your technical person to be "on alert" and immediately available on that first day.

- **Solve problems.** As best you can, find out if any of your participants are having problems. The problems usually come early in your course. If someone has a problem the first day and it is not fixed until later, it will have seriously negative influence on that person's learning, participation, and satisfaction with the course. So anything you can do to find out about problems, and then address them, is positive. Even if it is a technical problem with the person's own computer and totally out of your control, your response or understanding will be helpful to that person.
- **Recap the goals or objectives.** Begin by telling people what will happen in the course. Do this in a summary fashion. The complete goals and objectives and schedule will be in your agenda. But rephrase what will happen, make it pointed and forceful and positive. This will help people focus or refocus.
- **Invite interaction immediately.** As soon as you can, invite your participants to participate and contribute. Whether it is just putting in their name, or filling out a quick survey or question form— the sooner they are involved physically (typing, making a comment), the sooner they are involved emotionally and motivationally.
- **Give 'em your best stuff.** A rule of thumb for people attending conference sessions: If the session is not good in the first five or ten minutes, get up and walk out to another session, because that session is not going to get any better. You want to make a good first impression with your online course. The way to do that is to start off strong. Here are some tips for starting off strong.
  - Jump right into the content. The best way to start off strong is to get right into the content. Give them something to chew on immediately. Too many courses dilly dally around, talking about what people "will" learn in the rest of the course, without getting right to the matter at hand. Spend as little time as possible on the formalities, guidelines, and so on. Jump right into your content.
  - Give them your best stuff. Your first module, content or day online should be as strong or stronger than the rest of the course. If you can make a good impression on the first day, you've got them. If you don't, you could lose them. If you can bring out some of your best points, or a sample of the good stuff, that will get people excited. At a minimum, make the quality of your first day's content the same level as the rest of the course. And if you can add a little extra something that first day, do it.

- **Begin your dialogue.** Get into your discussion forum or chat room. Make a few comments. Get things going.
- **The more planning, the better.** The more planning, even rehearsing of the first day, the better. You don't need to rehearse or plan details for the rest of the course. But the first day of your online course is so important that it is worth writing out in advance your online comments, preparing a little bit more, doing a little bit more, for that first day.

Make that first day good, and you will be going downhill from there. If that first day doesn't go well, it will be uphill the rest of the course. The first day is important. Make it a good one.

Online Icebreakers

Online instructors report excellent success with online icebreakers at the start of the course. Here are some of the latest new online icebreakers teachers have shared:

- "Find someone who…" Give students a list of 10-20 items someone may have, and have them find a person with each of the items.
- "What you have always wanted to do." Each person shares his or her thoughts.
- "Find 3 things in common." Break the class into small groups and have them find three things in common.
- "Pair off — ask odd questions." Pair up participants. Prepare a list of odd questions for them to ask each other.
- "Crazy characteristics." From a list of 20 crazy characteristics, each student tries to find someone with that characteristic.

Weekly or Unit Welcomes

Do a separate and different "welcome" for each unit or week of your online course. It doesn't have to be long. It does have to be positive, enthusiastic and warm. The weekly welcome constantly involves your students, tells them there is something new, and solicits their enthusiasm.

Making Content Comments

It will be very helpful for you to make content comments in your discussion forum. The content comments from you help to tie things together and create a flow with your online course. They also tell your participants what information you value highly and what aspects of the subject matter they should explore fully.

Here are some tips on making content comments in your discussion forum or chat room:

- **Make your comments short.** From 6 to 8 lines of copy is a good rule of thumb.
- **Just do one thought per comment.** Don't try to string together more than one thought, concept, or idea in a comment. Focus each comment on just one thought.
- **Use highlighting techniques.** Feel free to underline some of your copy, boldface a few words, create a headline, or otherwise highlight parts of your comments.

Opening Rituals

I think "opening rituals" are also important to building community. Each individual reflects on and responds to the question. For example: "Fill in the blank: the thing I fear most about this class is..." — Chris Bakkun, University of Wisconsin, LaCrosse, WI

- **Don't think online.** Don't try to do too much thinking online while writing your comments. Composing a well-constructed paragraph of comment takes some forethought, and you should have a good idea what you want to say when you write it.
- **Feel free to do a draft.** Sometimes I type a comment and revise it before entering it online. Feel free to do a draft of your comments.
- **Focus on important issues.** Keep your comments oriented towards the important concepts or ideas in your course. Obviously you could go on and talk about a lot of issues online, but time and space is limited, so focus your comments on the most important ideas you want to convey.
- **Be careful about humor.** It is much harder to express humor online. Be very open about humor. For example, "This is a joke:..." Trying to be subtle with humor online will only confuse some of your participants.
- **Present new info.** If you have new or current information not contained in your prepared content or readings, using the discussion forum or chat room is a good way to deliver that recent or new information.

Initiating Interaction

As an online teacher, you will be making two kinds of comments in your discussion forum: 1) content comments; and 2) discussion comments. It is important you understand that discussion comments differ in style and substance from content comments. Content comments are meant to deliver information. Discussion comments are meant to encourage your participants to interact.

Here are some tips on initiating a discussion online:

- View the discussion as a conversation. You are a moderator or discussion facilitator. Keep the comments coming. Encourage people to interact.
- Get one or two people to make some initial comments or questions. If you just "open it up" to questions, you will see a blank screen for an awfully long time. Instead, arrange ahead of time for one or more participants to enter a comment or question to get the discussion going. Once you get two to four comments in there, you have a discussion going.
- When getting a question, first compliment the person on the question. Tell her or him, "Thanks for asking;" "Good question;" "Glad you asked that." Encourage people to ask. It is difficult to ask a question online — the person has to compose the question carefully and thoughtfully, and has to feel confident enough to post it.
- Allow others to respond to questions and make comments. Don't shut off discussion by making too authoritative a comment.
- Make sure someone responds to every comment. Every time someone makes a comment online, someone else should respond to it. Don't let thoughts or comments dangle unresponded.
- Look for connections. Try to connect several of your participants' comments or questions, citing similarities, or differences, among them. This creates a conversation, helps the line of thinking, and helps your participants put together a more cohesive reading of the discussion.

Moderating

Moderating a discussion online is one the key and critical skills you will want to develop as an online teacher.

Online, as in person, you will want to "listen" to your participants. Here are some tips:

- **Look to create "door openers."** When someone makes an initial comment online, ask if they would like to follow up with more information. "Tell me more." is one way to put it. Or you can ask a follow-up question.
- **Be neutral and nonjudgmental.** Russell Robinson, in *Helping Adults Learn and Change*, makes some good points we can adapt to the online learning situation:
  - Try to understand what is meant when the person makes a comment;
  - Don't try to contradict or refute a person's ideas too quickly;
  - Put aside your own views when responding to others;
  - Expect the participant's language to be different from your own;
  - Avoid negative feedback.
- **Help insecure learners.** Learners who lack confidence in themselves are common in adult learning. A good teacher needs to make the learning environment secure for these people. Building their confidence is not condescending; instead, it keeps their desire to learn alive.
- **Offer rewards.** Look for ways to reward your participants. The reward could be a positive comment. It could be an information 'gift,' such as a reference to a new link or site. Or it could be a physical gift, such as a free report or article mailed to the person. Rewards are positive reinforcements for the person and for everyone else in class as well.
- **Have expectations of your participants.** Australian Philip C. Candy, in his book *Self Direction for Lifelong Learning*, has this to say about enhancing security: "Educators who hold high expectations for their students tend to convey these through complex and subtle patterns of interaction, which commonly result in the learners living up to these expectations, and in the process, developing a more positive image of themselves."
- **Help with frustration.** Sometimes learners will demean themselves, professing inadequacy, frustration or outside interference. When the learner is unhappy about some situation, focus on how the student feels about the external situation, not the situation itself. When someone expresses frustration or inadequacy:
  a) don't contradict the person's views;
  b) don't use logical explanations;
  c) don't ridicule the person's view;
  d) convey your positive regard for the person.

- **Encourage shy participants.** Some participants prefer to be quiet and "lurk" and learn that way. Privacy deserves respect, but there are some overtures you as the teacher can make without intruding. Patience, invitations to make comments, and other strategies, like devising group exercises that involve making comments, can involve quiet learners without embarrassing them.
- **Avoid negativity.** Some of your participants will do or say things that are wrong. When someone does something wrong, don't punish that person by calling attention to the wrong comment or embarrassing the person. This is punishment and it is counterproductive. Punishment has inhibited more learning in a person's lifetime, and indeed throughout history, than any other single factor. Instead, use positive encouragement.
- **Steps in positive teaching.** In *Yes, You Can Teach*, Florence Nelson outlines the four steps of encouragement to maintain the learning climate throughout the class. Encouragement is not always effusive praise. Providing encouragement can be a subtle art, and it is a changing process depending on the needs of the learner. Nelson points to a four-step process that helps the learner become self-directed while lessening the role of the teacher. It illustrates that the best teachers are those who can step aside when the learner is ready. These are the four steps of encouragement:
  1. *The fundamentals.* In the beginning, effusive praise like "great," "wonderful," "keep it going."
  2. *Pleasing the teacher.* As they advance, let them know, "it is coming along well," "now you've got the right idea," and so on.
  3. *Pleasing the teacher and themselves.* Still further along, encourage them with comments like "Yes, that's it... how do you feel about it?" or "I can see some progress here, what do you think?" or "I'll bet you're proud of yourself."
  4. *Pleasing themselves.* And finally, when the learner is well along, you can say, "When you need help, just let me know."

Continuous Engagement

Mary Dereshiwsky, a professor at Northern Arizona University, has pioneered the concept and practice of "continuous engagement" as it relates to instructor involvement in online discussion. She writes:

" 'Being there' is an important aspect of the instructor role. It includes actively engaging with your students. Students will know when they log in that we have been there if they find a welcome message in their e-mail, announcement postings to get them started comfortably, and an updated syllabus for them to download.

"Continual engagement means keeping a close eye out for student requests for help. I create a *Questions and Answers* posting area in my online classroom. I encourage students to use it to post any questions about the course, syllabus, readings, and assignments. Just as in a traditional live and in person classroom, if one student has a given question, chances are that other students have the same question.

"In addition, continual engagement includes active instructor participation in discussion areas. You should regularly jump in with follow-up questions, quick summaries of emergent student thoughts on that issue, or even sharing your own experiences with that topic. If you care enough to get involved in the discussion regularly, your students will, too.

"Such continual engagement also means finding other creative ways to 'talk to' your students. Many of us post a weekly wrap-up announcement. I call mine *Taking the Pulse: Week* X. I also look for fun ways to 'talk' and 'be there.' One way I do this is by posting a cluster of interrelated positive-thinking stories, poems and quotes on a given theme twice a week.

" 'Being there' also includes prompt feedback on assignments. It's important, if possible, to tell them what they did right, as well as provide coaching-type comments on any areas that need improvement. Such continual engagement — taking the learning material in smaller, more manageable bites — makes the learning more understandable and likely to 'stick.' This is particularly true with relatively complex learning material such as research and statistics.

"Because of greater student engagement and continual learning, they will be more likely to complete their course and less likely to drop out in frustration."

By practicing such continual engagement in your online classroom, you are creating conditions for a maximally beneficial learning experience for your students, concludes Dereshiwsky.

Revitalizing Your Course Mid-way

Even the best online courses can experience complacency and boredom halfway through the course. "Keep up the momentum" urges Roberta Ross-Fisher of St. Louis, an online professor with Walden University.

Some of Ross-Fisher's top ways to revitalize your course mid-way:
- For one week, post a quote of the day and have students find quotes.
- Provide some clues, then have a "mystery guest" join your discussion board for a week.
- Create and host a jokes thread for a week.
- Create a mini-webquest for the week.

Chapter 15
Facilitating Online Discussions

Online, participating in discussions is not just good or helpful or positive to learning. Participating in online discussions is critical. It is essential. It is a must. And so a critical, essential online teaching skill is facilitating online discussions with your students.

In their excellent book, *Facilitating Online Learning*, George Collison and co-authors note, "An online community exists only if its members are active and posting. As a facilitator, you must draw all participants in and guide and focus the class discussions along constructive paths to learning."

Palloff and Pratt also point out that many instructors express frustration with student and teacher discussions online.

Netiquette

Netiquette is etiquette (good manners, acceptable behavior) for the Internet. In order to have a good discussion online, we have to have some guidelines, some boundaries, for conducting that discussion in order for the online conversation to be successful.

The problem is, we really don't know how to talk online. It is a totally new experience. Netiquette is a start at helping us to develop the skills to talk online.

So when your students go to make a comment during your online course, you will want them to follow good netiquette.

From several different sources, here are the best set of netiquette rules I can find relevant to learning online. Feel free to copy or post them for all your students. Netiquette rules for online classes:

1. Think of your comments as printed in a newspaper.

This insightful rule comes from Conrad and Crowell and is cited in Palloff and Pratt's book *Building Learning Communities in Cyberspace.*

Sometimes we think our online comment is like a verbal comment on the street. It won't be remembered and no one else is listening. On the contrary, everyone is listening. Your online comments can and are saved, so they can be remembered long after you have made them.

This isn't meant to discourage you from making online comments. Most comments you make won't be printed or distributed or used to embarrass you. But sometimes discussion online gets heated. If that happens, before you make an emotional or outrageous or sarcastic or personal attack comment online, think about whether you would care if it was seen in your local newspaper.

Wait to Respond

If I jump in and respond to a posting because I am as interested in interacting as the next person, I see the responses just end. There is an intimidation factor to being the instructor.

However, if I stay an observer awhile, most likely other participants will make the point that I wanted to make. And it is heard and understood much better coming from them than from me. — Sue McCullough, Southwest Texas State University, San Marcos, TX

---

2. Do not get emotional.

It is fine to express emotion. It is great to be passionate. But when your emotion overtakes you, take a step outside, take some deep breaths, and then return to your computer. Don't be overcome by your emotions.

3. Sign your real name.

When you are in a chat room on the Internet, and who knows who is there, it is fine not to use your real name. But when you are in an online course, you will need to use your real name. You probably won't have a choice; your online classroom software may automatically identify you when you post a comment.

4. Avoid self-centered comments.

If you have an idea, great. If you want to contribute to an ongoing discussion, terrific. But don't just tell others about your problems ("I'm frustrated;" "My audio doesn't work today") unless it contributes in some way to the class.

5. Avoid negativity.
You can disagree. You should disagree. You can challenge and dissent about ideas and the course content. But avoid becoming negative online. It will impact you negatively, hinder the class discussion, and may give the wrong impression of you to others.

6. No flaming, no all caps, !!!, ???
There is no need to be aggressive online.

7. Comments should be polite, understated, and use positive language.
Online we are very sensitive. We will get your point. Using bold, frank, overstated language conveys an emotional aggressiveness that hinders your message. Online, be polite. Understate rather than overstate your point. Use positive language. Your ideas will get a better reception.

8. Disagree politely.
When you disagree politely, you stimulate and encourage great discussion. You also maintain positive relationships with others with whom you may disagree on a certain point.

9. Don't disrupt.
If there is a dialogue or train of thought going on, join in. Participate, add to it. But if you have something entirely different to bring up, wait or post it in another area. Online dialogue is like conversation.

Teacher Netiquette

There are also some guidelines for you as a teacher in making comments online. Here is my list of teacher netiquette:

Make sure someone replies. Make sure someone replies to comments. You, as teacher, do not have to reply to every comment, but make sure someone in the class has replied. If not, wait an appropriate amount of time, then reply yourself to those postings with no reply.

Praise people for comments. Praising your students for making comments will encourage them to make more comments. Your praise does not always have to be effusive, and your praise does not have to indicate you

A new way of communicating is emerging, one that integrates pictures and words. This visual was designed by Julie Coates of LERN to encourage participants in an online discussion forum to make comments.

agree with the substance or the comment. "Interesting perspective, Carlos" is a neither effusive nor expressing agreement, but it is definitely positive reinforcement.

Dissent politely. Even more than your students, you will need to dissent very politely. As the teacher, your words "weigh" a lot more than your students'. The space between the lines is also a lot wider, so students may be trying to "read between the lines" more than with another student.

Thus, very gently dissent using subtle facilitation language.

Never blame or punish verbally. While I hesitate to use the word "never," this teacher netiquette rule is so very important. We unintentionally blame or punish in very subtle ways, and teachers need to constantly keep on the look out for this very common online mistake. Students take blame and even minor direct criticism very personally and acutely. Our job is to flame the fire of learning, not douse it. Be very careful here.

Encourage. Human beings hardly ever feel as though they are encouraged or praised enough. On the other hand, we usually think we encourage and praise others regularly. The lesson here is that we as teachers need to overdo the encouragement.

Encouragement can be expressed in many different ways, to individuals, to groups, and to the class as a whole.

Take the high road. There may very well be instances when you as the teacher are criticized in your online course. And there is a good chance you may perceive one or more comments as criticism when they are not intended to be so.

Either way, when there is debate, dissension, disagreement, criticism or things go wrong, it is very important for teachers to remain nondefensive and positive, to not return criticism or engage in negativity.

The Importance of Making Online Comments

Making online comments is an integral part of your students' online learning. There are many reasons why making an online comment helps your learners. Here are two reasons:

A. We learn from ourselves
We know your students learn from other. And from you the teacher, of course. But we also learn from ourselves. The next time you are in a discussion, think about it afterwards. Try to remember what you said. Most people can remember what they said. Then try to remember what

others said. You will remember more about what you said than about what others said.

We learn from ourselves. By making a comment online, your students will be learning from themselves.

B. Group learning

In group learning a discussion builds, a number of different people contribute and all of a sudden, a new idea, concept or thought emerges. No one person came up with the new idea. No one person could have come up with the new idea. Yet, there it is. It emerged, it was created, by the combined energies and thoughts of everyone participating in the discussion.

Treasure Hunt

For productive cybersurfing, do a treasure hunt or scavenger hunt online. Find an object or fact. — Merlin Wittenberg, formerly of Southern Adventist University, Collegeville, TN

Your students' comments, even one encouraging the discussion or agreeing, or rephrasing someone else's comment, contributes to group learning. And every once in awhile, a new idea will emerge that will excite and amaze everyone. Each learner commenting will have done her or his part in creating that new idea.

Kinds of online comments

There are many different kinds of comments your students can make online. Not all comments have to be brilliant, original, or brilliantly original. Here are different kinds of online comments. You may want to let your students know in advance what kinds of comments you value.

Content comments

These are comments focused on content originated by the person making the comment. They include original comments and additions to comments.

Original comments. These are statements that are, or appear to be, original with the person making the comment. We usually think of these kinds of comments as being the only valid comments in a discussion, but in fact only a small proportion of comments need to be original in a good online dialogue.

Additions to comments. These are statements that modify, expand upon, or add to an original comment.

Responsive comments

Responsive comments keep the discussion moving. Some kinds of responses are content-related, while others facilitate the discussion. Both kinds are very valuable.

Supportive comments. You don't have to respond to a comment with another great idea. It is helpful and positive just to make a supportive comment. You could write:

"Great idea, John."

"Very nicely worded comment, Charlene."

"Ramon, thanks for making that contribution."

In making your 'supportive' comment, you do not have to agree with the substance of the comment. Here are some neutral supporting comments:

"Very interesting point of view, Carlos."

"I had not thought of that, Cem."

"I wonder what other people think about that, Theo."

Supportive comments are very important in online discussions. Anyone can make them. Your students should be encouraged to contribute by making a supportive comment. It really does encourage others and keeps the dialogue going. And often it shows more knowledge, understanding and skill to make a supportive comment than a content posting.

Connecting comments. Now these are really great comments. Your students should get extra points for making connecting comments. A connecting comment ties together two comments that were made at different times. That is, the two comments aren't right next to each other.

Here's an example:

"Interesting thought, Isabella. Your idea might also relate to what Thomas was talking about yesterday when he said....."

You tie together two (or more) comments that are made at different times and often made about different points or topics. When you do that, you create a whole new perspective, idea or insight. Nice job. You can do it. So when you are reading comments and another comment made previously comes to mind, try making a connecting comment. It is fun and interesting and great learning. And the folks who made the two comments will be pleased too.

Responses. This is when you respond to an 'original' comment by adding to it, making another 'original' comment, or politely disagreeing with the first comment. Keep your thoughts positive. Make only one to two points in your response. Speak to the idea, not the person or the way it was said.

Follow-up questions. This is where you ask the person making the 'original' comment to clarify, expand, or rephrase their statement. This is a great technique. Some examples:

"Could you tell us more about that, Chuck?"

"How would you do that, Lisa?"

Initiating comments

These are comments designed to initiate or get the discussion going. Many times the teacher will make these kinds of comments, but you may want to encourage your students to help initiate discussion as well.

E-mail Experts

Have students e-mail experts and ask them a question or their side of an issue. You don't even have to ask for permission in advance. Many people are flattered to be asked. — Tom Conklin, Ottawa Carleton College, Nepean, ON

Introductory remarks. Usually done by the discussion facilitator or leader, but sometimes students can help the discussion early on by making an introductory remark. "Boy, I really enjoyed yesterday's conversation. I'm looking forward to today's discussion." is an example.

Discussion starters. Blatant appeals to get the discussion going. Usually done by the teacher or facilitator. "Okay, let's start by talking about..."

Transition comments. These comments come during an online conversation when a person wants to turn the discussion in another direction and uses previous comments to do so.

How to Disagree Online

You will probably want to encourage your students to disagree online. A big part of dialogue is disagreeing. But no online comment should be disagreeable. Tell your students:

Do not provide a negative statement about another comment.

Do not make a negative statement about another participant.

Instead, politely and nicely disagree. If you cannot disagree nicely, don't disagree at all.

Here's examples of how to disagree online:
- "My experience suggests…"
- "On the other hand…"
- "Looking at it another way…"
- "You may have a point, but…"

If your language, culture, or age group uses other words to disagree that are uniformly and universally understood to be "polite" and "nice," go ahead and use those words. Just make sure everyone knows you are not being hurtful.

Student Rules for Online Discussions

YES Rules.
- Yes, you can ask any question you want.
- Yes, you can reply and respond to any comment you want.
- Yes, there are no stupid questions.
- Yes, there are no right answers, and no wrong answers.
- Yes, you can politely and nicely disagree.
- Yes, every comment is valuable.

NO Rules.
- No negative statements about other comments.
- No negative statements about other participants online.
- Be careful about using humor.
- No acronyms that not everyone would understand and know.
- No 'inside' comments or clique communication.
- No using false identities unless everyone does.

Emoticons and Acronyms

Since it is difficult to convey emotion or tone in written comments, emoticons and acronyms have evolved in chat language. Collison, et al, define an emoticon as a keyboard symbol used to express a participant's emotion. An acronym is a form of abbreviation for a commonly used online phrase.

The most well known emoticon is probably :) which turned on its side is a smiley or happy face, representing the person making the comment was happy. Other variations include :-) and :^) or = :).

A frown is :(or :-(while a wink is ;-)

Some common acronyms include:

153

LOL. Laughing out loud.

BTW. By the way.

IMHO. In my humble opinion.

BRB. Be right back.

What is important for you and your students is to make sure everyone understands the emoticon or acronym. Create a glossary where everyone can add their favorites, or link to an emoticon web site.

Increasingly, you are likely to have students from different age groups, demographic groups, and different cultures. We embrace diversity, and we also have to minimize cliques, in-groups, and misunderstandings.

Here's an example. In all the books I've reviewed about online teaching, many have talked about and illustrated emoticons. But the examples have come from the authors' perspectives, which are almost exclusively adults over age 40. My 14-year-old son's most commonly used emoticon, therefore, does not appear in any of the books I've reviewed. His most commonly used emoticon is ^5, which stands for "high five," an expression meaning "way to go" or "I'm with you on that."

Now his favorite emoticon is (_8u(|) which is Homer Simpson, a popular animated TV personality.

His friend Bryn's favorite emoticon is ;-(or winking frown, which means "pretending to be sad."

To reiterate, be inclusive and learner-oriented by making sure everyone knows what the emoticons and acronyms mean.

Key Facilitator Roles

In their comprehensive work, *Facilitating Online Learning*, George Collison and co-authors offer six different roles for you as an online moderator, the "guide on the side."

They are:

1. *Generative guide*, where you "lay out a spectrum of current or possible positions taken to indicate avenues of questioning that have remained overlooked or unexplored."

2. *Conceptual facilitator*, where "key concepts in activities or readings may have been omitted, misconstrued, or overemphasized."

3. *Reflexive guide*, who "restates or recrafts... carries a sense of non-directive interaction, as... though the dialogue itself is goal-oriented."

4. *Personal muse*, where "you hold your own beliefs up to question.

There is a fundamental commitment to pragmatic, rather than argumentative, dialogue; there is no 'winner'."

5. *Mediator*, when "you redirect discussion away from defense of hardened positions and toward goals that are central to the interests of all parties."

6. *Role play*, when "you assume a voice appropriate to one of many roles... so, you can highlight or introduce, through characters or tales, key points that were omitted or that need reinforcing."

The authors also point to the weaving in of an online tone, such as nurturing, humorous, neutral, curious, or informal. The tone, almost always positive but varying in terms of approach, is determined by what you judge to be most appropriate and effective at that particular moment.

Collison, et al, argue against perceived negative tones, such as sarcasm or even saccharine comments, including playing devil's advocate, which they maintain can be better achieved through another more positive tone.

Discussion as Conversation

Online discussion can also be approached as a conversation. This author, for example, advocates discussion as conversation because it (a) leads to greater knowledge; and (b) enhances collaborative learning.

In moderating an online conversation, one attempts to encourage multiple messages exploring the same idea or topic, what Palloff and Pratt call a "volley of views." The more comments related to the same topic, and equally importantly, responding to and playing off of others' comments, the more likely the participants will enhance their skills in collaborative learning. At the same time, there is a much greater likelihood that the conversation, unlike individual postings, will lead to some new understanding or observation, as the whole (the online conversation) is greater than the sum of its parts (individual comments).

Facilitating online discussions at this point is both art and science. Palloff and Pratt point out that many instructors express frustration with their student and teacher online discussion. One reason for this frustration is that the study and practice of facilitating online discussions is so new. Because online facilitation is so new, we have much to learn about it. What seems clear, however, is that online discussion facilitation is an important and central skill for online teachers.

Time and Number of Comments

Palloff and Pratt recommend you suggest to your students they log on to the course 5 times a week. Logging on five times a week does not mean making a comment every time a student logs on.

Most experts say students in a credit course, where online participation is or can be mandatory, should make a minimum of one comment a week and preferably 2-3 online comments a week.

Most all online teaching experts, such as Palloff and Pratt, recommend you, as the teacher, should get into your online course and check on the dialogue a minimum of once a day, either making a comment or answering questions. Thus a minimum amount of time spent online is 15 minutes a day.

As to the number of comments the teacher should make, most online authorities agree that the teacher's comments should be in the minority, leaving the majority of comments to the students.

One of the biggest issues right now in teaching online is the amount of time a teacher spends online in dialogue. A few thoughts on that issue:

- If you are using e-mail for communicating with students, stop and instead use the threaded discussion software.
- Online discussion is good and positive and we should not do anything to limit or discourage our students from online dialogue and conversation.
- This issue is related to the issues of development time and teacher pay for online courses. If teachers received adequate pay for teaching online, the amount of time spent would be a lesser issue.
- There are ways to limit your time online, such as writing a response only once, developing a prepared list of responses to the most commonly asked questions so you can cut and paste when appropriate, engaging graduate students or even instructors from other colleges as discussion facilitators, and using your students to respond to questions and even help facilitate the online discussion.

Chapter 16
Evaluating Your Online Course

Now that there are tens of thousands of online courses and over a million people learning online, an emerging issue in the field is how to evaluate an online course.

Because making improvements and enhancements for your succeeding course offerings is imperative, evaluation is a significant process in the teaching of your online course.

While this book will provide a number of ideas for evaluating your online course, a panel of online experts cautions that we all have to take into consideration these dynamics:

1. *Outdated standards.* Most all of our evaluation standards for education are based on the needs and environment of the last century, the Industrial Age. Thus many commonly accepted standards may not necessarily be relevant for the 21st century and the Internet Age and the new knowledge economy.

2. *Online learning is new.* We have been practicing face-to-face education for hundreds or thousands of years. We have only been practicing online learning since 1994. This is the first generation of online teachers and learners, and we simply do not know enough yet.

3. *Rate of change.* Online learning is changing rapidly. If Moore's Law indicates that computer power and speed doubles every two years, online learning changes significantly every two years. If we did a review of the last ten years in online learning, we certainly would see major changes occurring every two years during that time span.

Thus, while we want to have quality assurance and standards for online courses, it may be premature to look for permanent standards by which to evaluate your online course.

You can, and should, look internally at your own online course for direction in improving the course. You can also look at other online courses for comparisons and helpful tips.

Every course should be in a continual state of improvement and quality enhancement. This does not mean you will need to redesign or redevelop your online course every time it is offered. You will probably want to improve 5% to 10% of your course each time it is offered. You will want to shore up weaknesses, but you will also want to respond to new technology and to continually raise the quality level of your course.

Colleague Meetings

Create your own small group of professors who are teaching online. This group tries to meet once a month to discuss issues/ideas regarding what is and isn't working.

Because of this group, our university came to us and asked us to create a student tutorial for Blackboard. — Amy Finch, Ft. Hays State University, Hays, KS

And as you enhance the quality of the course, student satisfaction goes up, and then you are able to gain more institutional approbation as well. As Dr. Mary Moretto has noted about her experience teaching online, "Once they see a success, they all want to be a part of it."

Three-year review

An online course should last three years. But best practices in online learning continue to change, be created, and be improved. So your course may need some substantial modifications or enhancements every three years. Best to check. Every three years, give your online course a thorough review.

Quality progression

Hopefully, you feel your first online course was "pretty good." But judging by the experience of experienced online teachers and experts, a retrospective look at online course quality progression is likely to be: first offering, awful; second offering, not so awful; third offering, not too bad; fourth offering, pretty good.

If you feel your online course is "really good," you probably are kidding yourself. The really good online teachers do not say their courses are "really good." The really good online teachers say they have a lot to learn and a lot to improve upon.

Select 1-5 improvements

You cannot improve everything on your online course all at once, nor should you. You have a limited amount of time and resources. The best time to think about what improvements you will want to make for your next offering is right at the end of your current online course offering, just before it ends.

Select from 1-5 things to improve, expand upon, create, or add for your next offering. Look at those things which a) will make the most impact on student satisfaction and participant learning; and b) are logistically feasible given time and technical resources.

If you select the top 1-5 enhancements each time you offer your online course, you will soon have a superior online course of which you can be very proud.

Value experience more

In receiving feedback, whether it be from your students, from other teachers, or from administrators, it is important to keep in mind that first-time online learners/teachers/administrators differ in some significant ways from more experienced online learners/teachers/administrators.

First-time learners and teachers often reflect views that are a result of their initial experience, and can be more a statement about the initial learning curve with online courses than about the course itself. For that reason, value the thoughts of experienced online learners, teachers and administrators more than those of first timers.

Evaluation Methods

Here are a number of methods teachers use to evaluate their online courses.

Student feedback

You will receive a number of impressions, reactions and suggestions from your students every time you offer your course. Be open to initiated student feedback. If three students independently provide the same feedback or offer the same observation, take that feedback seriously. It probably means many other participants also share that same view. On the other hand, if only one person has a given perception, it very well may be only that one person and not reflective of others in your class. Your students are probably the best source of clues to enhancing your course, and student feedback is an excellent evaluation tool.

Student behavior

Often overlooked, but even more important than what people say, is what people do. Analyze your student behavior online. Look at what they do, when they do it, how often they do it, and how they do it. Then study what they do not do (and try not to speculate too much on why they do not do it). Actions speak louder than words, and when you start studying your students' actions online, you learn a lot.

Some of the student behavior you can analyze: when they log on, how often they log on, what pages they most commonly frequent, the nature of their comments, participation rates in certain online activities. Student behavior online is one of the most important ways of evaluating your online course, and you should do some kind of analysis of what your students do for each and every course offering.

Student evaluations

Many online teachers conduct student evaluations of the course, either online or with a mail-in survey. Student evaluations should be done near the end of the course, but not more than a week after the course is over. The questionnaire should be short, not more than one page in length. Responses should be anonymous, with possibly an option for the student's name if there is a reason for knowing the student's name.

Do a few closed-ended questions (yes/no, Likert scale, etc.) followed by 1-2 open ended questions such as "What did you like best about the course?" and "What would you suggest I change about the course?" Thank them at the beginning and end for responding.

Do not go on a fishing expedition with your evaluation. Instead, know what you need to know. Select 1-3 things from which you want their opinions. When you get the answers to your most important questions, feel free to change the questions and ask something different in succeeding offerings.

Student evaluations are a common evaluation method for online courses.

Your own perceptions

At any point during the course, but particularly near the end, jot down some notes and thoughts about how the course went and what to change for next time. It may also be very important to write down what went well, and what not to change. Do not wait until the course is over to do this; even one or two days after the course the demands of your schedule will intrude and diminish your recall.

Teacher perceptions are a regular evaluation method for online courses.

Take an online course

One of the best ways to evaluate your own course is to take another online course. You will see similarities and differences. You will see what you like and what you don't like. You will experience online learning from the learner's standpoint. There are numerous low-cost online courses, many of short duration.

Teachers who take other online courses report the experience to be one of the most helpful in improving their own online courses.

Critique It F2F

Have students meeting F2F critique the online course. Then have your online-only students critique the course.

Peer review

Ask another online teacher to take a peek into your course, either before you offer it, during the course, or even after it is over. An experienced online teacher will provide positive and supportive comments, as well as make suggestions on where to improve.

Expert review

A number of organizations and consultants, such as the Learning Resources Network (LERN), do online course reviews as a consulting service. Since many online courses offered by your institution will be similar in nature and attributes, the review of one or two online courses will likely provide recommendations and analysis that is applicable to the rest of the online courses being offered by your colleagues in your institution. For that reason, getting an expert review might be a good use of resources and a win-win situation for both teachers and administrators in your institution.

Student advisors

There will be a few students participating in your organization's online offerings who are experienced online, knowledgeable, and enthusiastic about online learning. An excellent way to improve your course, and those of your colleagues, is to engage 5-10 of those students in conversation several times a year. Your conversation may be done individually. You may want to take them to lunch, or buy sodas later in the day. If you set up a "focus group" or "advisory committee," keep it informal with few if any rules or formality. You don't need any extra work, but you can benefit enormously from talking several times a year with a few experienced and supportive online learners.

Your report

Regardless of whether your organization requires it, you should do a one-page report for each online course offering you teach. Use the report to document the success of the course, record testimonials, report on class data and participation, and provide observations and recommendations.

Part V.
Learning Online

Chapter 17
Why We're Learning Online

In this section we look at how we learn online. Much of this section is taken from my book *Learning OntheNet*, which was written for online learners. In these chapters I will often refer to "you" as "you, the learner" rather than you as teacher. There are two reasons for this. First, as teachers we want to see our teaching from our learners' perspectives. Malcolm Knowles has called this approach "andragogy" as distinguished from "pedagogy." Andragogy is the study of how we learn. The second reason is that we are all learners. You, as a teacher, should be engaged occasionally as an online learner as well.

Online learning is growing by leaps and bounds. Every year thousands more online courses are being offered, and hundreds of thousands of more people are learning online. Online learning is happening in college, in the workplace, in high schools, and in continuing education programs. Soon it will be everywhere.

There are some immediate and practical reasons why we're learning online these days. Traditional classroom learning, which we will call in-person or face-to-face learning in this book, is starting to show some limitations. The cost of travel, time involved, need for quick updates and information, offerings at only one day and time, and only one location, are a few of the limitations.

But there is something bigger going on as well. Our society is moving rapidly from an industrial or manufacturing-based society into an information or knowledge economy. Online learning responds to an information or knowledge-based economy. It has certain characteristics that fit in well with where our society is going technologically, business-wise, information-wise, and educationally.

Eventually, we will all come to understand that learning online is actually better than face to face for cognitive learning (the neck up), that learning which involves data, facts, information, and critical thinking. For other kinds of learning, face-to-face learning will be better.

Your Reasons to Learn on the Net

You may have one or more reasons to learn online. Here are some:
- *Subject not available locally.* The subject you want to learn is not available locally.
- *Learn from the best teacher.* Your online course instructor may be an authority or expert.
- *Convenience.* You have a changing, busy schedule.
- *Cost.* When you figure in time and travel, or maybe a babysitter, online is financially more feasible.
- *Other participants.* You want to network, share ideas, and learn from others in your online course.
- *Fun.* Online learning is exciting, new, different, and in many ways, just plain fun.

You may have some specific, immediate outcomes you want to achieve. They may include:
- Get college credits.
- Pass a test at work.
- Get advanced placement.
- Prepare for an entrance examination or application.
- Remain up-to-date with changes in your profession or field.
- Be able to use a new technology, hardware or software program.

All reasons to learn on the net are good reasons. By being able to state your reasons for learning online, you are better able to assess your accomplishments and feeling of satisfaction at the end of your online course.

Are You Right for Online Learning?

In preparation for this section, I worked on a quiz for about six months to help you determine whether you are right for online learning.

I analyzed other similar tests, came up with 99 questions, refined the questionnaire, and came up with the final version, which I regard as just about perfect. Get out your number 2 pencil and get ready. Here is the quiz:

Question 1. Do you want to learn online?   __ yes __ no

That's it. That's the only totally valid question. We have many other questions that could indicate the hurdles, the likelihood, the ease with which you will learn online. But there's really only one question that matters: do you want to learn online? If you do, then you can overcome all the barriers, all the issues, all the challenges of this new and admittedly imperfect learning method. And if you do not want to learn online, it doesn't matter what computer you have, how young you are, how many times a day you chat online, you still won't have a positive experience.

Online Readiness Quiz

An online course readiness quiz that is objective and helpful. Check it out at http://www.ltcc.net. — Lake Tahoe Community College, South Lake Tahoe, CA

People who learn online span a large age range, from 15 to 50 to 80. People in different generations have certain learning characteristics, says Julie Coates, author of *Generational Learning Styles*. Keeping in mind that you are an individual and the following descriptions may not apply to you at all, it is nevertheless interesting if not helpful to get an idea of how people in different age groups may approach online learning, says Coates. Here's her brief summary of generational online learning.

Ages 15 and under. The Net generation have the online skills built into them. They were born with technical aptitude and attitude. In their play, online chats, and web explorations, they are regularly building the online skills required to learn and work online.

Ages 16-25. You are on the cutting edge of the computer revolution. Your age group is more likely to be able to take apart a computer and put it back together than any other age group. You are technically able. Some of you are more into hardware than younger folks, who are more into software, because the hardware advances were made while you became intrigued with computers. You, or your friends, are some of the brightest techies around right now. You have or can readily adopt the skills needed to learn online. You will want to learn online, because it will be an integral part of your work life for the next 40-50 years.

Ages 25-35. You are well aware of where the future is, and all the changes that are going to take place. But you've been in the workforce awhile and have had to play some of the old twentieth century games to get along. And you may be in an organization that hasn't changed much yet. You're not as savvy technically as those younger than you, but you are light years ahead of anyone older than you. Many of you like the technology and embrace and are good at it. You will be in the leadership in helping your organization transition into the Internet Age. You not only will be good with online learning, but you may be the most likely to consider teaching and developing online courses as well. Go for it.

Mentor for Skills

I collaborated with faculty from another Kentucky university last summer to design an online physical assessment course. We had cognitive content and testing online, used a textbook as written material, gave internet links as additional resources. For clinical skills, it was an expectation that each student find a "mentor" in their clinical practice setting to teach/validate clinical skills. Mentors signed an agreement, gave some biographical info about themselves, and might have had a short phone conversation with the lead instructor of the course. They snail-mailed completed competency forms back to the instructor. Worked great. — Connie Siefker, Murray State University, Murray, KY

Ages 35-45. Well, if you are 35-45 you've got a little unlearning to do. Learning online won't come naturally. You can see the need for it. You can see the necessity for it. You may want to learn online. You may want to learn online anywhere from mildly interested to desperately deeply desirous to learn online. There will be some challenges, some internal dissonance, and you will feel lost sometimes. But the retirement age is now a moving target, and it ain't getting any closer, so you will definitely be living in exciting if chaotic times over the next two decades. Might as well jump in now and get ahead of your peers.

Age 45-55. The dilemma is most profound. You not only like face-to-face learning, you believe in it. You are not sure when you are going to retire; it might be in ten years, it might not. And for a majority of you, "retirement" means a second or third career, if part-time. You have few of the skills needed for online learning, but you are also part of a generation of lifelong learners, so you have the skills to learn how to learn online. Learning online will be a challenge, but a lot of you like challenges, like mental challenges, and like change. You are most likely to have the most caution, criticism, and be aware of the shortcomings of the current state of learning online. But when you commit to it, you will be "dangerous" online (a positive term meant to convey deep involvement).

Online Project Idea

To get students to work together online I presented a group project that required students to use WebCT Bulletin Board. I asked the class to create web pages that provided information and annotated hyperlinks that they found useful in their MBA program for each of the functional business areas — accounting, human resources... Students were to decide who would handle each area, e-mail their web pages to a coordinator who put the final project together, ask/answer questions. Students enjoyed working on the project and the final result was a web site with useful info and sites for all of our MBA students. — Susan Simmons, The Citadel, Summerville, SC

Age 55-70. Online learning has little or no impact on your work career, even if you are starting a new job. You can take or leave online learning. Go with your gut instinct. Online learning will likely lengthen your life. It will offer you opportunities to learn things you cannot find in traditional courses, study tours or lectures. You should not give up your involvement with in-person and face-to-face learning. The rewards of online learning will be internal, and extending your likely life span.

Age 70 and up. There are those around you who have chosen not to go online. And there are many of your peers who have decided to go online. As you know, they communicate with family, friends and youngsters online. They may shop online. If you want to take on learning online, it will bring a whole new perspective to your already full life, keep you hopping, and probably extend your life, all other things being equal. Others have no expectations of you, so anything you do online will exceed your goals and be a big plus in your life. If you want to learn online, you have the most mental freedom, and the least to lose. Go for it.

—Greg Brecht

Chapter 18
How Online Learning
is Different

One of the first questions students usually ask me when taking one of my online courses is, "Where's the video?" While they may be expecting a video, the deeper issue is that they expect online learning to be familiar, to be like watching television or sitting in a traditional classroom lecture.

Learning on the Internet is different.

There are three major differences between learning online and traditional classroom lecture classes:

1. Learning online is active and self-initiated
2. Learning online requires self-discipline
3. Learning online is results-oriented

By comparison, traditional classroom lecture classes are:

1. More passive and responsive
2. Guided by external discipline
3. Attendance or activity-oriented

This is not to say that the three characteristics mentioned above for the traditional classroom lecture class are bad. For the 20th century and the Industrial Age, these characteristics were good and were necessary in order for someone to function effectively in the workplace.

To be an effective employee or worker in the Industrial Age, you needed to listen and then respond to your superiors, generally the leaders of the company. You needed to be guided by external discipline, as exemplified by your supervisor. Everyone had a supervisor. It was important to get along with your supervisor. You had to show up on time and put in your time at work, generally forty hours a week. The company

169

depended on you to show up on time, and to put in your appropriate number of hours per day and week.

A major role of education is to prepare people for the workplace, and to respond to the needs of society. So education did its part and prepared students for the workplace of the 20th century by instituting external discipline (the bell), requiring people to show up (taking daily attendance) and to listen and be responsive to the teacher.

In the 21st century, the Information Age, the Internet Age, these characteristics are not helpful or positive. They do not help make you a more effective worker in the information sector, which is the predominant employment sector of this century.

Instead, to be an effective worker you need to be: a) self-disciplined, and b) active and creative and participatory. We don't care how many, or how few, hours it takes to do the job, all we care about is the outcome.

Thus learning online is consistent and supportive of the very traits and skills that we as workers need to be effective in the world of work. Learning online is not just different because it is different. And it is certainly not different because it is isolated or inferior or next-best to being in a classroom with a live teacher. Learning online is different because it responds to the very different requirements of the working environment of the information sector and this century.

Here's how learning online is different.
1. Active and self-initiated.

You will need to be active in your online class. You will need to sit down and reach out; be aggressive, assertive, and directive of your learning.

No one will tell you or make you go to related links that will extend your learning.

No one will know if you are excited by a particular unit or module and you would find a more advanced or detailed unit much to your liking. You will have to sense that yourself and act on it.

You will need to participate in online discussions. This is not an option. It is not something you can choose or not choose to do. It is not dependent on your preferred learning style or whether you are "shy" online. You simply must be active in online discussions to learn.

2. Self-discipline.

Learning online is hard work. And what is worse, there is no one to monitor your work, supervise your work, gauge your energy or time put into your work.

Self-discipline will be one of the hardest aspects of learning and working in the Information Age to instill, acquire, and grow. And of course it will be one of the most rewarding aspects of your learning. And it will be one of the essential keys to success in the work world of this century.

3. Results-oriented.

In the Industrial Age much of success was related to showing up, being present, and putting in time. And that was true. But in the world of work in the Internet Age, just showing up is meaningless. The only thing that matters is whether you can produce, whether you can produce results, whether you can get the job (project) done.

Learning Space

Not only should you tell your learners how to rearrange and modify their physical learning space around their computer, but we also have our students report to me on what their physical space looks like. — Gail Sammons, University of Nevada-Las Vegas, Henderson, NV

Online, it is the same way. You will not get extra points for logging into your course ten times more than other students. Simply logging on will not make you smarter. Simply clicking on the audio lecture will not mean you are actually listening to it and can pass a five point quiz about it.

Online, regardless of whether you spend a lot of time or a little time, what matters is whether you can pass the quiz, whether you have learned, whether you have the knowledge skill.

If you have to put in more time than another person, that doesn't matter either. If it takes you twice as long to learn something, you are still just as smart.

But just showing up doesn't count anymore.

You Will Feel Differently

You may feel very differently about your learning experience online. This is natural. It is because:
- Learning online is a very different experience.
- We don't know a whole lot about learning online yet.
- Learning online is only half of learning; there are some things you

Act One:
Intimidated

Act Two:
Isolated

Act Three:
Intrigued

Act Four:
Involved

Sometime first-time online learners have to go through several stages before feeling positive about online learning.

cannot experience online that you can experience in an in-person group meeting.

Here are some of the emotions you may experience, especially in your first online course:

1. Confused
2. Lonely
3. Challenged
4. Distracted
5. Unsatisfied.
6. Out of sorts.

Make Comments a Discussion, Not a "Test"

I like the idea of posing questions by the instructor with an alias, too. I know that my students are sometimes reticent about speaking out for fear of looking "stupid." When another "student" asks a question, it lowers the stakes for being wrong. It's like it becomes a discussion, rather than a "test."
— Arnie Pfieffer

Confused.

When you walk into a traditional classroom, you know where to sit, where the teacher will sit or stand, and what some of the rules are. Online, there is no industry standard for a virtual classroom, you don't always know where to go, and we're still making up the rules. If you are confused:

a) Understand that others are confused also.
b) Ask the teacher for clarification, guidelines, and expectations.
c) Ask the teacher where you are supposed to go, what you are supposed to do.

Lonely.

When you take a class online, others are there with you, but you cannot see them, often cannot hear them, and it is harder to get to know them.

Here's what to do:

a) Understand that others are lonely also.
b) See if you can trade pictures, set up personal web sites with information, or just mail each other something about yourselves.
c) Find one to three online buddies. Create a 'study group' that is also a friendship group. Use it to get to know others in your class.

d) E-mail one or more of your classmates and ask if there is a time when you can telephone and talk.
e) Find the two closest people in your class and try to meet somewhere, sometime, during the course of the class.
f) Ask your teacher if there are other ways you can connect with others in your class.

Challenged.

The online class work may seem huge and overwhelming. After the initial rush or excitement wears off, there are still many days left in the course and a lot of work to do. Here's what to do:

a) Understand that others are challenged too.
b) Create a schedule for studying online
c) Do not put in too much time in the beginning. Pace yourself. You are in a marathon, not a 40-yard dash. You can put in too much time and effort early and then not have enough energy for the rest of the course.
d) Write a "to do" list. Your 'to do' list has chunks of assignments, not big ones. Read 10 pages; listen to ten minutes of the lecture; study for 15 minutes before taking a break. Celebrate the little victories. After you have read ten pages, take a big pen or marker and check that off your list, then declare victory with a few sips of your favorite beverage.
e) Ask your teacher for guidance and suggestions.

Distracted.

You may feel distracted when you are trying to learn online. A lot of different demands come at you from all angles.

Here's what to do if you are distracted:

a) Create a time devoted only to your online study.
b) Modify a place to create an environment devoted only to your online study.
c) Let others know you are not to be disturbed.
d) Allow a few days or weeks to get accustomed to your new learning environment. You won't sit down to your computer on day one and be able to full concentrate. It takes time to adjust.

Unsatisfied.

You may feel unsatisfied with your online class experience. There are many reasons why online learning may be unsatisfying. Your teacher has not been teaching online for very long (no one has). You have not been learning online for very long. Your fellow participants have not been learning online for very long. We are used to allocating blame for unsatisfying experiences on others, especially the teacher.

Do not be too critical. Shift responsibility from others to yourself. Instead of pointing out the problems, become part of the solution. On this issue, you have to own up to your own feelings of dissatisfaction and simply do something about it for yourself.

Self-discipline and Motivation

Online learning takes more self-discipline and self motivation than traditional classroom courses, especially for first-time online students. Online teacher Tracy Helixon says: "Spend some class time discussing this issue directly." She notes that in teaching online, student motivation "was by far my biggest challenge."

Here's what to do:
a) Document for yourself what you like and don't like about the experience.
b) Write something about your experience.
c) Make a list of positive suggestions for next time.
d) Try to do something to make the situation better.
e) Don't blame others, including the teacher, even if they are worthy of blame.

Out of sorts.

It's hard to explain. You're not unsatisfied, you're not lonely, you're not frustrated. You're just out of sorts.

Welcome to the world of online learning. This is natural. This is normal. Your teacher feels a little 'out of sorts,' and the author of this book feels a little 'out of sorts' learning online.

Here's what to do.
a) Acknowledge the dissonance. Revel in the dissonance. Well, maybe not revel, but you can "get into" the dissonance. Recognize your feelings (to yourself, you don't have to bare your feelings to others) about learning online. It's not always easy. It takes some effort. It is different.
b) Now get into it. Figure out what's going on, how you will deal

with others online, and how you can get to know others online and form online relationships. You will be able to get to know your fellow students online, sometimes in more personal and intimate ways than if you were in a traditional classroom together. There is an interconnectedness online, and there are things you can say and do online that you could not say or do face-to-face. If you are taking the course from a distance, you may not even have been able to take your online course at all.

c) You will move from feelings of uncertainty to being intrigued and involved. That ambiguity will remain, but you will begin to feel comfortable with the initial ambiguity of cyberspace. You will be an online learning pioneer.

Chapter 19
How Young People
Learn Online

Young people (those under 30 in the year 2002) have more of the online learning attributes than people older than 30. It doesn't mean they will get better grades online, or that older adults cannot learn online. But it does mean that they come to situation with a better aptitude for the skills needed to learn online.

Those born after 2000 will already have these aptitudes built into their systems. For those of us who spent most of our lives in the last century, we will want to unlearn as much as we can and adopt new ways of thinking about our learning when we go online.

Here are some of the learning characteristics of young people online:

1. Technology is good. Almost universally young people see technology as good. Adults often are cautious, wary or see the downside of the Internet. For young people, the Internet is good. What the Internet can do might be scary, but one need not be afraid of the technology, nor see it as posing uncontrollable risks or dangers.

Unquestionably, if one sees the Internet as good, then one will be more able to learn effectively online.

2. Learn by discovery. The "discovery" method of learning is different than how adults have been taught to learn. The "discovery" method is more immediate, more task- or outcome-driven, seeks relevance, and involves trial and experimentation (discovery).

In one of my online courses, an adult participant exasperatingly exclaimed about the numerous participant comments in the discussion forum,

177

Chat is natural.

For young people, online chat and discussion is more natural than for adults.

"There's too much information here." That is exactly the point of why online learning is necessary: the world has too much information. And if you do not have any idea of what you want to learn, you will be deluged by too much information. To reiterate the Cheshire Cat's response to Alice: "If you don't know where you want to go, then any road will be fine."

To cope with too much information, adopt the discovery method and find out what you need to know when you need it.

If we expect to start at the beginning, and wind up at the end, we will become hopelessly bogged down with too much information.

Collaborative Learning Insight

When my 12 year-old is on the computer, she generally has a friend or two sitting next to her. How silly of me to set up a computer area with one nice chair by it for use. When I work on the computer, I am isolated and have the door closed. She comes in and chatters and I became frustrated. She becomes confused because she feels she is helping. — Marlene Tucker, Salt Lake Community College, Salt Lake City, UT

---

3. Scan, don't read. This is a skill we need to apply online when we begin to learn by discovery. We are actually very good at it when we read a newspaper. But somehow we don't apply the same approach to our learning.

Online, scan, don't read. Use the built-in keyword search software capabilities to find what you are looking for.

When you read a book, read. When you are on the Internet, scan.

4. Chat is natural. Typing in comments online comes much more naturally to young people than it does to adults. Only about 35% of adults feel comfortable making comments online, while about twice that percentage (close to 70%) of young people feel comfortable making comments online. And this percentage will grow to 90% or more.

Making comments online is not only critical to your learning online, it will also be required in the near future as we begin to work online.

5. Netiquette is important. Young people understand that in order to have successful conversations online, there has to be some rules, an element of politeness, and concern for others. Since they are young people, they may break those rules or test the limits, but they know when they are doing that as well.

Interconnectedness is different.

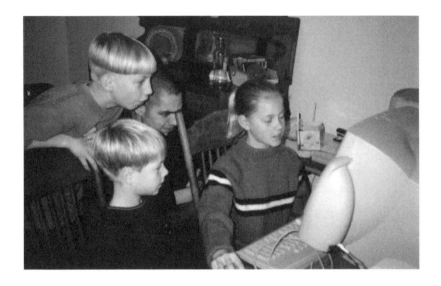

For young people, the Internet and online learning is more of a social experience than for many adults.

6. Learning is also visual and auditory. More than adults over 30, who learn primarily by text, young people are more visual learners. We will see much more dynamic visuals, including animation and simulations, in online learning in the near future.

7. Trust your judgment online. There used to be 'gatekeepers' in the world of knowledge. They could tell you what was right, what was wrong, what was reasonable, what wasn't, what the most outstanding novels of a particular century were, and so on.

But on the Internet, anyone can say or post or declare anything. The Internet is full of false or misleading information. It is full of opinion. There are a lot of intentional spoofs. And there are some heretical ideas that most of us would consider false today that in 25 years will be almost universally acclaimed as true.

So who do you trust online? Primarily, you have to develop the skill and the assurance to trust your judgment online. This involves developing a few skill sets. A good technique, recommended in Don Tapscott's *Growing Up Digital*, is to "consider the source." Researching the source of the information is one such way to help you develop your online judgment.

8. Face-to-face is good too. Adults over 30 were brought up believing in either/or. Something was either true or false, either yes or no, either right or wrong, either red or blue. Adults over 30 often place technology and online learning in that either/or situation; online learning is either good or bad; they see themselves as either online learners, or in-person learners.

Young people see technology as being in balance with face-to-face encounters and learning. For them, online and off-line is both/and rather than either/or.

So face-to-face learning is valid, good, and has an important place in their lives. They are not spending 98% of their lives on the Internet. They see more balance in life than that.

9. Interconnectedness is different. Adults over 30 often view computers and the Internet as isolating individuals, and separating them. For them, face-to-face encounters establish relationships and interconnectedness.

When I visited my home town recently, I went to the public library. Downstairs, in the adult section, there was one adult per computer on the Internet. When I went upstairs, to the children's section of the library, I found two, three, sometimes four young people on a computer on the Internet. While adults see computers as isolating people, young people

181

Face-to-face is good, too.

do not experience or behave that way. The Internet is a socializing experience for them as well. They play together online.

Likewise, they have a better sense of how we are interconnected on the Internet. We exist in relationships, in a community, relating to each other. It is a new way, an unfamiliar way, for most adults over 30, but that interconnectedness is there. Young people see relationships and interconnectedness online.

10. Learning is collaborative. For adults, learning is very much an individual activity. For many young people, learning is something to be done with others. Young people are pioneering this more collaborative way of learning. Often one will see two or even three young people at a computer.

11. We learn from other learners. Young people, more than other generations, are pioneering new ways to get knowledge and information from other learners. In sharing music files, this is often called peer-to-peer (P2P) file sharing. The concept of P2P easily can be transferred to the learning setting where learners learn from each other.

This author calls such learner-to-learner activities L2L, while Conrad and other educational experts also encourage students to learn from other students instead of always relying on the instructor.

Generational Differences

Julie Coates, in her pioneering book *Generational Learning Styles*, says that generations learn differently. There are currently five generations currently engaged in learning: Silent Generation (born 1930-1945), Baby Boomers (1946-1964), Gen X (1965-1980), Gen Y (1981-1999), and Gen Z (2000+).

You as an instructor also teach based on the learning style of your generation. Many readers of this book are Baby Boomer or Gen X instructors teaching Gen Y and Gen X learners. Thus, understanding the generational learning characteristics of the generations you are teaching is important. It is even more so because of the generational sensitivity of the online environment.

"The day of the multi-age classroom is here, and the issues of how to manage diverse populations in the workplace are upon us," writes Coates. For teaching Generation Y, Coates recommends more experiential learning, lots of structure, using technology, incorporating games, offering multiple options for performance, and other teaching strategies relevant to Gen Y.

—Greg Brecht

Chapter 20
Tips for Online Learners

Some 25% of our learning is affected by the physical environment, according to a study by the U.S. Department of Education. Of course, the physical environment impacts our learning in a classroom. But the physical environment is at least as important in affecting our learning on the Internet.

One of the things we have to do in learning online is to control and manipulate our physical environment. If you don't control the physical environment when learning online, the outside interference will not just inhibit, but maybe prohibit, your learning online successfully.

Where to Set Up Your Computer

If you have any opportunity to buy a laptop computer, do it. Laptops are the ideal computer for learning because you can change your location and create the proper online learning environment for yourself.

If you cannot get a laptop, see if you can move your computer to a better learning location.

For example, I like a great blues radio program on Friday nights. I can only get it on the Internet, since the radio station is out of my area. I have found that I cannot listen to the station in my home office. It is a 'work' room, not a relaxing room. So I unplug all the computer hardware and lug it upstairs to my bedroom, set it all up again, modem in from the phone line — and it is all worth it.

Here are some locations to think about for your online learning place:
- *Bedroom.* Usually the most relaxed and restful room in the house, think about setting up a little desk in the bedroom, or just studying from your bed.

- *Kitchen table.* If you don't have lots of folks roaming through the house, the kitchen table often has a nice view out the window.
- *Home office.* Make sure you can create a learning environment out of your work environment. If you feel edgy, guilty about work, or out of sorts, this might be the wrong room. Or spend ten minutes 'redecorating,' getting rid of work files, and putting on music, setting up an aroma, and bringing out your favorite (or second favorite) beverage.
- *Office at work.* This is a tough place in which to learn. You will definitely have to be aggressive about creating privacy, about getting work files out of sight (and thus out of mind), and creating a learning environment for yourself.

Enhancing Your Online Learning Room

Whether you engage in your online learning from your home or from an office, here are some tips for enhancing your online learning room:

Close the door

Close the door. Don't schedule or even allow conversations or meetings to interfere. Tell the kids not to bother you. Put a sign on your office door if you need to. Reduce and eliminate interruptions at all costs.

Get enough light

If there is not enough light, or the right kind of light (sunlight versus artificial), you will not learn effectively. How the light in the room falls on your computer screen is important. Get the right amount of light.

Manage screen brightness

Use the screen brightness control knob on your computer to get the brightness of your monitor just right.

Consider a large monitor

You will learn more if you have a larger monitor. A 19-inch screen, for instance, will enhance your learning over smaller screen sizes.

Turn off e-mail

Don't be distracted by e-mail alerts that pop up and say, "You have new e-mail." Turn that new e-mail message off.

Play music

Music may help your learning. Or not playing music may help your learning. Or white noise to block outside noise pollution may help your learning. You know what works. Select the kind of music that will settle you down, help you relax, and enable you to concentrate.

Have a beverage

If you enjoy a beverage, whether it is water, coffee or a soda, go ahead and bring a beverage to your computer. A little beverage will help you focus and learn better online.

Online Office Hours

I have met some instructors who actually have specific office hours for their online courses. Each day a student can log on at that specified time and post messages to the instructor — and will get immediate feedback. Also, if they need to talk privately with that instructor, they can either e-mail or call at that time. This may not work for some students; however, the students will know of a specific time to try to get in touch with their instructors. — Sissy Copeland, Piedmont Technical College, Greenwood, SC

A little food

A little food will help you at various times of the day. But a lot of food will inhibit your learning, lessen your concentration, and make you sleepy. Have a big breakfast. But be wary of having dessert with lunch if you want to learn online in the early afternoon, and avoid a heavy supper if you are learning in the evening. Try healthy snacks instead.

Try aroma

If you like a pleasant aroma or smell in the room, then try it with your online learning. A candle, a little vanilla on a light bulb, a warm slice of apple pie in the room, or steamy herbal tea are all options.

From conversations with frustrated online learners, much of the problem stems from not setting the right physical environment. Enhance your learning by creating a physical environment that is pleasant and pleasurable. When you do, your online learning will be much more successful.

Set a Time and a Schedule

It is very important to set a time of day and days of week in which to study online. There's actually two schedules you need to create:

1. Time online. This is when you go online and participate in class discussions, download information, and otherwise learn online.
2. Time offline. This is for reading the textbook, reviewing notes, writing, and other study activities with the computer turned off.

The best way to stick to your schedule is to print out a daily or weekly schedule, and fill it in with a pencil or pen. Then keep it in a visible place where you can remind yourself to stay on schedule, and where you can waive the sheet in front of others who try to knock you off schedule.

Budget a set number of hours per week you want to spend on your online course, and then block out the time on your daily schedule sheets.

How Much Time to Budget

Online courses take about as much time as face-to-face courses. Just because a course may be running continually for a week or more does not mean you have to be on the Internet continually.

Generally, you should not spend more than one hour a day online with your course. If your online course runs from 6 to 16 weeks in length, then you might want to log on 2-3 times a week.

A typical three-credit college course online takes about the same amount of time as a traditional three-credit class. According to Dr. Rita Conrad, a three-credit online course would typically involve the following hours for a student:

40 hours	Reading
20 hours	Online dialogue with teacher and other students
30 hours	Doing assignments and projects
30 hours	Studying and assessments (tests)
15 hours	Management tasks
135 hours	Total time for a three-credit online course

If your online course is awarding Continuing Education Units (CEUs), the number of CEUs awarded indicates how much time you should spend online and offline studying. Ten hours of study and participation equal 1.0 CEUs. So if an online course awarded 1.5 CEUs, you would want to spend 15 hours total studying and participating.

If it is not clear how much time you should devote to your online course, simply ask your teacher.

Time of Day

Study online and offline when you are at your peak learning time. If you can't, then study when you have the time based on your work schedule. Here are some times of the day when people go online to learn:

Early morning. 6 am - 9 am — before going to work, or at work before the work day begins. This is a good time of day to learn online if you are an early morning person, or can become an early morning person.

Morning: 9am - noon. For a number of people, this is their peak learning time. It is also peak work time for a lot of people, so the two may conflict. If you are able to take the time off, this is a good time for learning online.

Afternoon: Noon - 4 pm. The idea is good — get your work out of the way in the morning, study in the afternoon, but the reality is often harder. If you are planning on learning online in the afternoon, a) beware of a heavy lunch; b) get some exercise, take a walk, or otherwise refresh your energies before going online; c) make sure all that work stuff and files are put away or stashed underneath the desk; d) stay in touch with your feelings as the afternoon progresses. A number of online learners are more irritable and experience greater frustration online in the afternoon, particularly from 2 pm to 4 pm. If you feel yourself becoming frustrated, stop and rethink your learning times.

Early evening: 6 pm to 9 pm. Another good time for folks. Usually they have changed environments (from work to home) or changed routines. Things have settled down. A good time to go online.

Late evening. 9 pm to midnight. Many people get tired during this time period, but if you have the energy, the outside world interference certainly dies time during this time of day. If you are a late evening person, this is a good time to learn online.

Overnight: Midnight to 6 am. If your biological clock has you running strong during these hours, more power to you — go for it. If you are not naturally or regularly up and feeling great during this time, it is probably a poor time to push yourself to learn online. Of course, if there's someone half-way around the world online at the same time, this can be an exciting time online unlike any other time of the day.

Weekends

If weekends are your time to go online, great. Weekends may be different schedule-wise, but your biological clock runs the same on weekends as during the week, so stay aware of what times of the day are best for you.

The Top 20 Most Important Things to Do to Prepare for Your Online Course

Here are the top twenty most important things to do to prepare for your online course. Use this list as a checklist for your next online course.

1. Decide if you want to learn online.
2. Tell yourself again your reason(s) for learning online.
3. Be able to accept your role as a pioneer in online learning. Tell yourself you won't expect everything to be perfect.
4. Find your 'passion' on the Internet. Log onto the Internet several times to research or explore your 'passion' (hobby, music, sports team, news source, etc.)
5. Accept that you will feel differently in your online course.
6. Select a place to learn online.
7. Make 1-3 enhancements to your physical learning space.
8. Select a time of day to learn online.
9. Write down your weekly online learning schedule.
10. Get a techie.
11. Get acquainted with a virtual classroom. Take a noncredit, low-cost (under $100) online course if you have not taken an online course before.
12. Download the software/plug-ins you need for your course. Test them.
13. Read a short book, or take an online course, about how the Internet works.

14. Listen to something over the Internet.

15. Visit an Internet chat room or bulletin board.

16. Make a comment online.

17. Respond to someone else's comment online.

18. Take a quiz, survey or poll online.

19. Think of one way to connect with your fellow students face-to-face. OR Think of one way to connect with a fellow student via distance other than e-mail or the Internet.

20. Don't delay. Go for it. Enroll in your online course and follow the instructions. Relax. Enjoy it.

Part VI.
The Future
of Online Learning

Chapter 21
Work in the 21st Century

Your online students probably have some immediate and specific reasons for taking a course online. But there are some long term reasons why online learning will continue to grow. That's because online learning is central to our new Internet Age or Information Age economy.

The skills your students acquire about how to learn online will be the very same skills they will need to prosper in the workplace of the 21st century.

Here's a look at how work will change between now and 2020, thus making online learning central to work in the 21st century.

We are now in a new economy, called the Information Age or Internet Age. It began in 1991. That was the first year that businesses spent more on computers and software than they did on other capital expenditures. It was also the year that Tim Berners-Lee invented the World Wide Web. And it was the first year in which advanced societies had more information than could be feasibly received by any one individual (sometimes called Infoglut).

Between 1920 and 1991, advanced societies were in the Industrial Age, the age of factories and offices.

And before 1900, we were in an agricultural or Agrarian Age, the age of family farms. In 1900, 50% of people were employed on farms. After 1900, the percentage of workers employed on farms plummeted to where only 1% or so of workers in the United States today are working on a farm.

Between 1900 and 1920 society was in transition, moving from the Agrarian Age to the Industrial Age. Between 2000 and 2020 society is in transition again, moving from the Industrial Age to the Internet Age.

During the 20th century, the Industrial Age, the predominant sector of the workforce were factory workers in the industrial or manufacturing

Industrial Age to Information Age

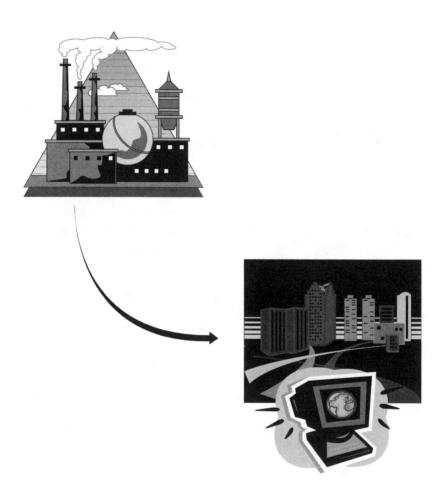

Our society is moving quickly from the Industrial Age of the 20th century to the Internet Age of the 21st century.

sector. But the percentage of workers employed in the manufacturing sector has been declining to where in 2000 only 34% of workers were employed in the manufacturing sector. That percentage will continue to decline steadily during the course of this century.

What means for countries like the United States, the so-called industrialized nations (they will have to come up with another word now), is that there will be fewer and fewer opportunities for workers in the agricultural and manufacturing sectors of the economy. Other countries such as Mexico will have a manufacturing sector and agricultural sector employing a significant percentage of its workers. But for the United States, Canada, Britain, Scandinavian countries, Australia, New Zealand, and possibly other European countries, there will be few if any job openings in manufacturing, just as there have been almost no job openings in the 20th century in farming.

The predominant sector of the workforce will be Information Age workers, sometimes called knowledge workers.

Thus, for people entering the workforce after 2000, or remaining in the workforce after 2010, the jobs that pay well enough to support oneself and one's family will be in the Information sector as knowledge workers.

Job openings and job opportunities for knowledge workers will continue to grow, and the nature of work for knowledge workers will change dramatically.

Two interrelated forces are driving the need for more knowledge workers. They are:

Growth of information. The growth of information has not lessened the need for more information, but created a greater need for information. Businesses are changing so rapidly, the market is shifting so quickly, the need for quick turnaround, flexibility and speed so great, that more knowledge workers will be needed to maintain business profitability and competitiveness.

Existing knowledge workers will have to keep up with the changes in information, thus spending more time in learning to remain productive. You may spend as much as an hour a day in learning if you are in the workforce after 2010, about half of that learning time spent learning online.

Moore's Law. Moore's Law is also driving our work lives. Moore's Law was created by Gordon Moore, who worked for Intel, a computer chip maker since the 1960s. Sometime in the 1970s he discovered that computer chips were doubling in power and speed about every 18-24 months. Experts can verify that over the past four decades and predict

Intellectual Capital

Intellectual capital (your brain and your thinking ability) is the only competitive edge for most companies and organizations in the Internet Age.

that Moore's Law will be in place at least until 2020. That means a computer chip in 2010 will be one thousand times faster and more powerful than a computer chip in 2000. And that, says British Telecom researcher Peter Cochrane, means rapid societal change.

By 2010, Cochrane says that objects will communicate. Light bulbs, refrigerators, pace makers, will all have computer chips that will tell you when a light bulb will burn out, when a refrigerator will need to be fixed, and when you should go to a hospital to check on your heart.

Some 95% of phone communication will be machine to machine, with no human involved, notes Cochrane.

And sometime shortly thereafter, computer power will exceed brain power in computational power.

These two forces will make knowledge workers all the more needed, valued, and productive. Knowledge workers — those who work with their brains — will increasingly work from home or wherever they are or choose to be. And the most valuable resource to knowledge workers is time, which will go up dramatically in value.

Cochrane says that there will be two classes of people in an Information Age society. There will be those who spend time to save money, and those who spend money to save time (knowledge workers).

Knowledge workers have different work needs than workers of the industrial age. Here are some of them:

Time is valuable. In fact, time is so valuable that knowledge workers will do anything it takes to preserve and use their time wisely. Time is the only resource that knowledge workers have. Wasting time is simply unacceptable.

The average knowledge worker produces between $200 and $500 U.S. (In 2001 dollars) per hour for her or his employer. The knowledge worker doesn't make that much. But that is the amount of income generated for the organization.

So the knowledge worker's world revolves around maximizing time.

Balance is important. For every high-tech innovation, there is an equal high touch reaction, says futurist John Naisbitt. While knowledge workers may work long hours, not every hour is devoted to work.

Family and leisure time becomes more important. Knowledge workers spend time with community organizations, and they spend more time in nature and in parks.

The Organization Chart is a Pyramid

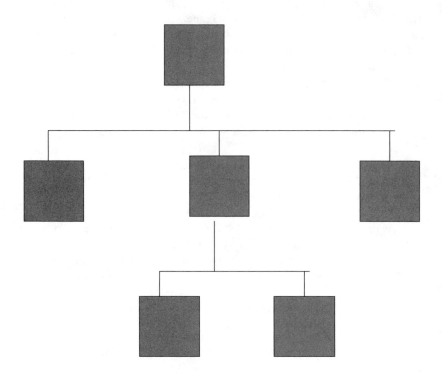

Work is an activity, not a place. British Telecom lead researcher Peter Cochrane says that work is an activity, not a place.

Since knowledge workers use computers, and increasingly laptop computers, they can do their work wherever they are most productive. Increasingly, that means working at home or in one's local neighborhood rather than commuting long distances to an office.

The numbers of people working from home are increasing by the millions each year.

Your web site becomes your office. All organizations, led by business, will be managed and run using an Intranet, a password protected area on the Internet. So your web site will become your office.

These virtual offices will perform all of the functions we do now in a physical office, only better. Communication, meetings, supervision, work: it will all take place in your virtual office on the web.

Other implications. There are many more implications for lifestyle change in this century, which is fun to speculate about but not critical to our discussion here. But some of them this author foresees include: denser communities linked to downtowns and airports by light rail; fewer cars and less time spent driving; home deliveries of numerous basic commodities and services; reurbanization as office buildings downtown become apartment buildings; and more time spent travelling, primarily using light rail, fast trains, and airplanes.

People who work from home (or as my 25-year-old son prefers, the neighborhood juice bar), are more productive, work longer, and require less supervision than people who work in an office. People who work from home also have more leisure time, and more time for family and community.

Cochrane says that soon work will no longer be a place; it will be an activity. As you are or becoming an online learner, you can see that education is no longer a place but an activity as well.

How can a person working at home work longer and have more leisure time at the same time? People working from home save an average of two hours a day commuting. Spend an extra hour working, and an extra hour for leisure or family, and it is a win-win situation.

Thus, the number of people working from home is growing steadily. Companies are beginning to allow it, and some even encourage it. But around 2009, businesses — led by the Fortune 500 — will be mandating that employees work from home.

Organization as Network

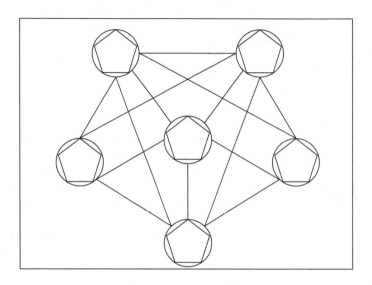

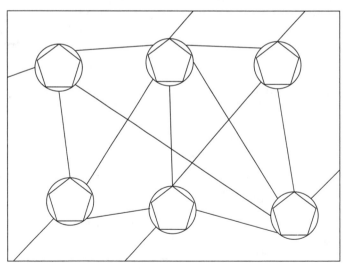

The likely structure for business and organizations in the 21st century is a network. Two examples are shown above.

Here is why business will be sending its employees home around 2009-2010:

1. *Save money on office space.* This is the least important reason, but it adds up to millions of dollars a year for a larger company.

2. *Save on supervision.* This is an important concern. Businesses can no longer afford to have their best employees spending a significant amount of their time just making sure that other employees are doing their work. Valuable staff time spent on supervision must necessarily decline in order for business to make the best use of its most talented people, and to remain competitive.

As we will see later, supervision will be done much more efficiently and effectively online by using a virtual office or company Intranet.

3. *Continual employee turnover.* My father, who worked in the information economy as a newspaper man, worked for one company for 40 years. Employees today change jobs about once every 5-10 years. But in 2010 and beyond, people will view jobs more like "projects" and have a new job on average once a year.

The needs of business will change so rapidly that flexibility in workforce will be a plus for the business. And your needs as a worker will change so that you will benefit from the new experiences, locations, contacts, and lateral or vertical advancement that annual new projects bring.

So by the time a business gets the office repainted for the new employee, puts a sign on the door, puts her birthday date into the staff celebration schedule, and does some staff bonding to welcome the new person, she will be on the way out to her next job/project.

4. *Save two hours a day per employee.* Now we are talking big dollars. The average worker spends two hours a day commuting to work. Except in the Washington DC area, where they spend 82 hours a year stuck in traffic— not going anywhere, just stalled.

The average worker is worth between $200 and $500 an hour to a company. That's not how much you make, but it is how much the company can gain in income per hour of your time. On average, let's say that is $50,000 a year per employee. If a company has 100 employees, that's $50 million a year.

And we're not even talking about the stressed-out lowered productivity level that a person arrives at the office with after a commuting experience.

Growth of Information

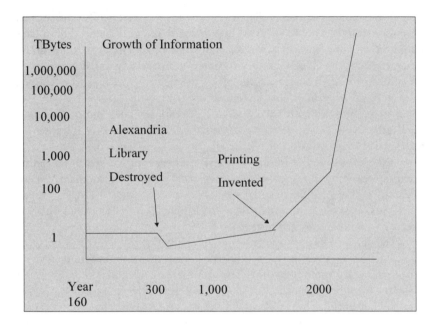

This is simply unaffordable. Two hours a day is 25% of a knowledge worker's time. And that makes the difference between profit and loss, competitiveness or uncompetitiveness.

5. *The best people won't move.* Compounding the issue is the biggest reason of all: the best people won't move. Companies will need the best people to remain competitive. The best people don't have to move. In fact, their high level of output and outcomes would probably fall if they were taken out of the environment in which they are most productive. So you don't really want to move productive people anyway.

Without the best people, companies fall behind. Getting the best people to move, whether it is to another city, another country, or simply another suburb or another six blocks, will shift from being difficult to becoming next to impossible. The best people will simply work for businesses where they don't have to move.

This is the single greatest reason why companies will send their workers home. So they can recruit and retain the best workers, regardless of where those people live.

6. *Young workers will simply refuse.* Around 2010 the Net generation, the baby boomlet 80 million strong, will begin moving into the workforce. They will be Net savvy. And they won't commute.

The Net generation, the first generation in history which cannot remember a time when there was not a computer in the house, will simply not understand and not be willing to spend two hours a day to get to something (a laptop) that they have in their own apartment.

We know this because it happened before. In the middle of the twentieth century, people used to go downtown to watch the news. They would go downtown to the movie theatre and, before the movie began, there was a newsreel with the latest news. Until television was invented, when people said, why should I go downtown to watch something that I can get in my living room? The same will be true for work.

Work for knowledge workers will be done online using a laptop or similar device. Companies will build virtual offices with password protection, often called an intranet. At the time of this writing, some 90% of the Fortune 1000 had an intranet already. And by 2010 companies will realize that a worker can be better supervised using an Intranet than supervision in-person. And that online communication and 'meetings' are more productive and accomplished more quickly than face-to-face

Chip Prices

Today		2010	
$1	embedded	$.10	embedded
$10	watch	$1	watch
$1,000	computer	$100	computer
$10,000	top-of-the-line computer	$1,000	top-of-the-line computer

Source: Gordon Bell 1998

staff meetings. And that people working from home work longer and are more productive (read profitable). And more.

When you work from home, as I do, you find that time becomes much more valuable. Your work is judged by results or outcomes, not by the amount of time you put in. So if you do your project in half the time — good for you, you get paid the same amount and you have more time to go out and play, or work on another project and make more money.

Time spent commuting, shopping, unnecessary meetings, quickly becomes wasted time. You will want to spend more time either working, or enjoying life (leisure, family, friends, community, service).

To maintain your skill set and your knowledge level, you will engage in regular learning, sometimes online, sometimes face-to-face. But if you can save time in travel, staying overnight, and learn more quickly by learning online, you will do it. Because time will be even more valuable than it is now (if you can imagine that).

When you work from home (or the backyard, or airplane, or neighborhood office, or...) you will want to shop online and have it delivered, instead of spending time travelling to the store to buy toothpaste. You will want to walk 3-6 blocks to stores, community centers, and hangouts. You will want to take a train or light rail when travelling because you can work online, or read, or do something else either more productive or more enjoyable than driving. You will spend less time with the television. You won't enjoy driving as much. Many of you will want to balance the high tech life with an increasing amount of time spent in nature, in parks, in the great out-of-doors. As you read your newspaper or favorite magazine over the next few years, you will notice more and more stories about these growing trends. They are all part of moving our society, and your work, into the Internet or Information Age.

Online learning matches the requirements of the work world of the 21st century. This is why elementary and secondary school age children will begin learning online, and why higher education will prepare students for the work world by incorporating online learning.

Once in the work force, the typical knowledge worker will:

- *Spend up to an hour a day learning.* You might not think of it as learning because it will become so prevalent and permeate the work world and your daily routine. But you will learn online at least a half-hour a day. The other half-hour will be spent in semi-annual conferences, institutes or other in-person learning.
- *Focus on your specialty.* Your learning will focus on those things

you need to know to continue doing your job successfully and enhancing your career. So we will not all be taking "customer service" or "quality control" courses online. Each of us will be engaged in very specific customized learning tailored to the needs of our own job.

- *Prepare for your next job.*

All of which is to say that your students' current involvement in learning online will not only be beneficial to them in the short term, but in their future as well.

When you learn online, you develop the skills of self-discipline, making online comments, retrieving information, learning by discovery, scanning when you need to, reading when you need to, focussing on outcomes and results rather than putting in time, and more. These are the same skills your students will need and value as a knowledge worker in the 21st century. Online learning will be an ongoing and integral part of their future, and the skills learned in online learning will be transferred and utilized in their work life.

Chapter 22
Life in the 21st Century

The driving force in society for the 21st century is the computer chip and the Internet. For the 20th century, the Industrial Age, it was the automobile and the factory that made the automobile. One hundred years ago the richest men in America were John D. Rockefeller, Andrew Carnegie, and others involved in oil and steel— the stuff that made automobiles and made them go. Today the richest people in America are Bill Gates, Paul Allen, and others involved in computers and the Internet.

Just like the automobile shaped society in the 20th century, the Internet will shape society in the 21st century. The automobile was not just a means of transportation. It created suburbs, the nuclear family, greater freedom for women, shopping malls, community colleges, and consolidated school districts. The factory that built the auto created an organizational structure based on the command and control pyramid of hierarchy. The computer chip and Internet will have a similarly dramatic and significant impact on all aspects of life in the 21st century.

We don't know yet all the ways the computer chip and Internet will influence our lives. But we do know already that the computer chip and Internet increase the need for knowledge and information. The need for current information, knowledge, and knowledge skills is so great that lifelong learning will be at the center of society, including the workplace, for at least the next hundred years.

To remain competitive and profitable, every business will increasingly rely on updated knowledge and skills from its people. So we know now that lifelong learning, which has already grown tremendously in the last 25 years, will increase even more dramatically in the years ahead.

Lifelong learning is the engine that runs the Information Age.

To understand how the Internet is changing work, life, and education in the 21ˢᵗ century, we go not to Bill Gates's house, not to Silicon Valley, but to Kansas, and to Frankfort, Kansas, in particular.

I have driven through Frankfort, Kansas, many times. It is about eight blocks long. There's nothing really there. There's a public school. The only store that's ever been open when we've driven through is a combination convenience store, gas station, soda grill, grocery store, and youth center.

But a few years ago my brother, who lives in Texas and frequents antique shops, found a brochure from 1907 for a department store in Frankfort, Kansas. When he gave me the brochure, I could not believe that Frankfort, Kansas, ever had a department store of this magnitude. It was called Helleker's Department Store. It had more clothing and goods than any store that you could possibly imagine in 1900 in the town of Frankfort, Kansas, population 1,200. The store was like Nieman and Marcus. There was probably not a store in Washington DC or Los Angeles or even Chicago that had more than Helleker's in Frankfort, Kansas.

At Helleker's, they had 150 ladies' capes. They had shoes that are the best line on earth. They had shoes for men, boys and youth, women, misses, and children. Here's just some of the shoes they had just for infants: Baby Budd shoes; infants' silk trimmed moccasins; infants' soft-solid button shoes. Now you can't buy shoes at all in Frankfort.

Soon after receiving the brochure I decided to go to Frankfort again, because I wanted to find out why there was a department store there in 1907, and what was going on in 1907 in Frankfort. So I called up the library. It was closed. I called the police station. I got an answering machine. Finally I found someone and they told me about June, the librarian. I called June and she invited me to the Frankfort library that afternoon.

The Frankfort library today is a one-room library. I said, "I'm interested in knowing about the department store that was here in 1907." And June said, "Which one?" It turns out there were four department stores in Frankfort back then.

So I asked her what life was like in Frankfort in 1907. She said Frankfort in 1907 had six banks and four department stores. There were two opera houses. Frankfort had an African-American community. It had a racetrack. It had a newspaper. Not just a newspaper, but a daily newspaper. In the daily newspaper you can see the train schedule of the daily train going from Frankfort, Kansas, to New York City. The bankers were millionaires who imported marble and stained glass from Italy for their homes. It turns out there were thousands of people who came to Frankfort to do business, shop, and attend cultural events.

Frankfort was a pretty special place, I thought. Well, I asked June, where was the next town where they had an opera house and millionaire bankers, and she said, "Eleven miles away in Blue Rapids, Kansas."

It turns out Frankfort, Kansas, was not unique. This is how America lived. This wasn't just Frankfort. This was all of America. Because in the early 1900s, a majority of people in society farmed. We were in a rural, agrarian economy. A large farm back then was 80 acres.

When you fly over the country, look down on the ground and you will see little squares. Those are each one square mile. It is called a section. There are 640 acres to a section. Today Kansas farms and ranches are thousands of acres. A 10,000 acre farm is not unusual.

But in the early 1900s, a farmer had 80 acres if he was lucky. And so all around Frankfort were hundreds and thousands of people who were farming, and they all came to Frankfort to buy goods, be entertained, and visit. And then something happened. They invented the automobile and they invented gasoline. The first automobile was sold in 1896, the same year that *The Wizard of Oz* was written.

Two years later, in 1909, the first automobiles rolled into Frankfort on a cross country tour of small rural towns. Within ten years Frankfort, Kansas, was in decline. The opera houses closed. Helleker's went out of business. The millionaire banker went bankrupt and went back to Scotland where he died penniless. People left town, moved to the big city, went to work in the factories.

Frankfort did nothing wrong. Instead, the automobile, gasoline, the factory, and the Industrial Age changed everything about the way we live. But I don't think people woke up in 1915 and said, "My grandfather farmed. My father farmed. I think I'm going to go to the factory and assembly line in Kansas City or Omaha and get a job."

I don't think that's what happened. I think a more important use of gasoline-powered engines than the car was the tractor. Because the reason the largest farm was 80 acres was because that was what a horse could plow. With a tractor you could plow more, and better. You could plow 160 acres, 320 acres, 640 acres, 1,280 acres and more. The tractor could plow deeper than a horse-drawn plow, so there was more yield per acre, which meant there were fewer farms.

So the invention of the tractor caused people to have to move off the farm and into the cities. Today we would call it "downsizing." They had to get different jobs. And a whole way of life changed.

Think of your area of expertise, your 'business' of teaching a course if you will, as an 80 acre farm. We, as teachers, are all running little 80

A page from Heleker's Department Store brochure in 1907.

Beautiful
Spring and Summer
.....Suits
At $15.00 $20.00 and $25.00

You must see these suits to fully appreciate them; to catch the faultless style, the superior workmanship and fine quality of fabrics. Made of fine Panamas, in blacks, browns, blues, a complete showing of the various grays, and in mixed Novelty Cloths.

A page from Heleker's Department Store brochure in 1907.

211

acre farms. And the tractor— in the form of the Internet— is about to change how we teach and learn.

So I tell you the story of Frankfort, Kansas, because once again life is changing. By 2020 we will no longer be living in the Industrial Age of the 20th century. Work, life and education will be very different. Part of this new world of the 21st century will be the growth and proliferation of online learning and teaching.

Chapter 23
Education in the 21ˢᵗ Century

In 1900, most children were educated in the rural, one-room school-house. Within twenty years, the rural, one-room schoolhouse went into steep decline and became virtually extinct by the middle of the 20ᵗʰ century.

But the rural one-room schoolhouse was not "bad" education. One of the foremost adult educators of our time, Jerry Apps, was educated in a one-room schoolhouse. He authored the book *One-Room Country Schools*.

The one room schoolhouse disappeared because it did not meet the needs of the 20ᵗʰ century, the century of factories and offices.

One hundred years later, today's education is going through a total overhaul again. Between 2000 and 2020, all educational institutions will become web-based.

Educational institutions today were devised for the Industrial Age, the century of factories and offices. They have these obsolete characteristics:

- *Bricks and mortar.* In 1900 at the World Exposition the first school architecture plans were released, plans which are still largely followed today. Factories and offices depend heavily on buildings, so too did 20ᵗʰ century education.
- *Bells and tardiness.* The 20ᵗʰ century factory and office depended on people showing up on time and working eight hours a day. So schools installed bells and tardy slips to prepare youth to work in factories and schools.
- *Age-grades.* If you are 12, then you are in sixth grade. While 19ᵗʰ century schools allowed students to progress at their natural speed, 20ᵗʰ century schools required uniformity in curriculum, ages and grades.
- *Input measures.* The eight-hour day, 9 to 5, was the measure of

The rural one-room schoolhouse met the educational needs of our agrarian society in 1900. But our educational system had to be redesigned for the 20ᵗʰ century.

(Original painting by Julie Caffee of Elkhart, Kansas)

worker performance in the last century. So school and education measures were based on time spent, not on outcomes measured.

Here are characteristics educational organizations will adopt for the 21st century:

Education as an activity, not a place

If work in the 21st century becomes an activity, not a place, then education will too. Learning, even at the elementary school level, will be seen to be allowed and encouraged to take place in many different settings, and at different times.

The last century notion that education takes place in one building will disappear. On-site learning will take place in several different locations.

Web-based

Education organizations will be web-based, not building-based. Communication will take place online among teachers and between teachers and students. Homework, information, quizzes and much more will be online.

Less time-specific

School hours are based on factory hours. But educational research has proven that early morning is one of the worst times for teenagers to be at school. In this century, education will be less time specific. Students will have more fluid schedules. Schedules will match their individual physical, cultural, and personal characteristics to maximize learning.

Less external discipline

The factory and office of the last century depended on supervision and external discipline to function effectively.

Workers in the 21st century will have little or no supervision, and have to depend on self-discipline.

To prepare students to become more self-disciplined, schools will need to discover ways to help students develop self-discipline.

Individual learning plans

Individual learners will work with teachers to help create, and then monitor and modify, individual learning plans. These online plans will tell the learner, teachers (and in the case of elementary and secondary school, the parents) what knowledge skills the learner has acquired and what still needs to be learned. Called "Learner Management Systems"

Factory or School?

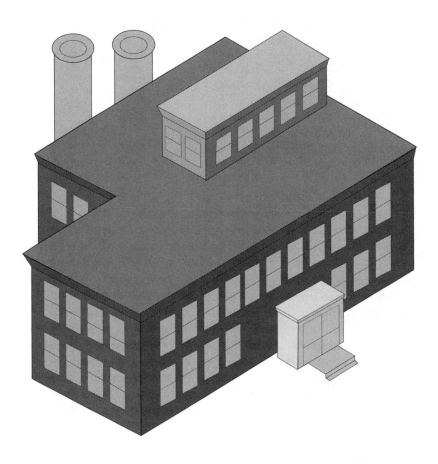

Is this a factory or a school? Schools in the 20th century were based on the factory because the primary purpose was to prepare people for work in the factories and offices prevalent in the last century.

software in the business sector, this software is applicable and relevant to formal education as well. This software will also be used for individual course completion, providing an objective record of what homework has been turned in (posted) and when, to aid in communication.

Elementary schools

Some online learning will begin in the earliest grades, beginning as play and games. Face-to-face learning will predominate. In later grades students will begin learning at home and in other locations. More online learning will be integrated into the curriculum.

Buildings decline

Fewer buildings will be needed. Buildings are huge unsustainable costs. Only space which is utilized for 12-18 hours a day will be able to justify the cost. F2F classrooms are more likely to be carpeted, with chairs in a circle to facilitate discussion. With learning online growing, and lectures disappearing, space needs will decline.

Online and F2F

Students will integrate online learning and face-to-face (F2F) learning. Students will engage in both, and many courses will have both an online component and a F2F component.

Guide on the Side

Face-to-face teachers will cease being the "sage on the stage" and instead become the "guide on the side," facilitating learning and helping students to learn. A knowledge of the student will be more important than a knowledge of subject matter for this new teaching role.

Part VII.
Strategic Planning
for Online Courses

Preface to Strategic Planning

This section on *Strategic Planning for Online Courses* is intended for experienced online teachers and administrators. It is not intended for first time online instructors. This information is advanced and controversial.

This section is written for online instructors and administrators who want to position themselves or their departments/colleges/institutions for long term success in the 21st century.

The previous sections of this book contain information and techniques endorsed by many, if not most, online experts and authorities. You can see by the many references that these sections are a collection of thinking from the best minds in online learning.

This section is very different. You do not need to read this section to teach online. You do not need to agree or accept any of the ideas in this section in order to teach online. If any of these ideas create a problem for you, simply ignore this section.

Warning: Information in this section is advanced, controversial, and unique. You do not need to read this section in order to teach online.

Information in this section is original to this author. For many of the ideas expressed in this section, I am the only online authority advocating or forecasting them.

If you do read this section, you will need to: 1. Separate the ideas in this section from the techniques in the previous sections. 2. Understand you do not have to agree with the ideas in this section. 3. Agree to consider the ideas in this section and accept that they are legitimate and have a firm foundation of rationale and fact behind them.

Recently I had the pleasure of having dinner with three colleagues who are outstanding authorities in online learning. At one point we began discussing an issue for which I have a particularly unique perspective which is not accepted by others in the field. Suddenly, one colleague turned to the other two and explained "Bill's a visionary."

This was a very diplomatic way of stating the following with regard to my views:

- They are big picture.
- They are long term.
- You do not have to accept them.
- Most people don't agree with them.
- You should, however, hear these views out, consider them, and see them as legitimate and worthy of consideration.

At the same time, please understand that these views are not forecasts or projections of the future. Richard Thieme, the outstanding technology futurist from Milwaukee, once said, "I am not a futurist. I simply explain the present to the 98% of people who are not there yet."

So, the ideas in this section are not forecasts, projections, or futurism. Instead, they represent the present reality for me personally, for my organization, and for a growing number of others. My colleague Julie Coates says that this is actually the past, that the transitions, realities described here have already happened.

So while this may seem "futuristic" to you, for me I am simply describing something that has already happened and that is a present reality for a number of us.

Chapter 24
The Economics
of Online Courses

Your online course is not just an educational experience, it is also an economic activity. For the past one hundred years, educational activities took place within the paradigms and parameters of the Industrial Age. Those economic paradigms and parameters are changing as we move further into the Information Age. So it will be increasingly difficult to make your online course be successful using the assumptions and rules of the last century. Increasingly, you will need to position your online course using the rules of the Information Age. Here are some of the economic principles of the Information Age.

The Shift from Products to Markets

In *The One to One Future*, the best marketing book of the last decade, business authors Don Peppers and Martha Rogers, urge us to "manage your customers, not just your products."

"In the traditional marketing organization, products are managed, and customers are simply counted at the cash register."

They recommend we stop managing products — read courses, seminars and other educational programs. Instead, Peppers and Rogers suggest we manage customers — read participants, learners, students. Here's why.

In the old world of the 20th century, we had a product orientation. We start with a course and then we offer this course to people. The problem with this scheme is that the real force here is people, our markets, our target audiences.

With a product orientation, we are unable to foresee, plan and adjust our programs to the changing interests and demands of our learners. We will only know it when enrollments decline. And then we won't know why. In today's world, we have a people orientation. We start with our markets, our target audiences. Then we build courses around each different market segment. In this way, we become responsive to our learners, to people instead of programs. We are then better able to do research, listen to our customers, understand their needs and adjust our offerings accordingly. We are also able to go after new audiences and look for new opportunities.

Segment Your Audience

"We serve everyone" is no longer a successful way to look at your potential audience. When someone asks you who would be interested in your course and you answer, "Anyone," that is a risky proposition.

It assumes there is one audience, one general public. But audiences are being defined in more specific terms, more distinct from each other, more defined by demographic characteristics than ever before. So there is not one audience, there are many.

There are no longer "nurses." There are now rural school nurses, emergency room nurses, large hospital nurses, small hospital nurses. Every audience is being divided up into ever-smaller segments.

In order to offer your online course successfully, you will want to define your audience by segment. That means using some kinds of demographics to define the people who will be most interested in your online course.

Here are some of the most commonly used demographic variables used to define target audiences today: geography, age, occupation, education level, job title, size of company, sex.

Look at the demographic characteristics of the people presently enrolled in your courses, who are your current customers, or are members of your organization already. These are most likely the characteristics of your potential participants in your next online course.

Look at several different market segments in choosing what audiences you want to target.

Traditional Boundaries Are Disappearing

The traditional boundaries between organizations and businesses are disappearing. The Internet has destroyed these boundaries.

Geography is no longer a boundary. It used to be that your organization, your business, was defined by your city, your county, your state, your region, or your country. You may still define it by geographic boundaries. But others on the Internet do not recognize geographic boundaries. They will serve anyone, anywhere.

Geography will no longer protect your course from the competition.

Time and place are no longer boundaries. Along with geography, time and place used to be boundaries. We would offer something that is convenient to our customers. We were closer to our customers. We were more available. Today, with the Internet being open 24 hours a day, 365 days a year, anyone on the Internet can be accessible to anyone much more easily than a physical location can be convenient. Time and place are no longer advantages to you.

Affiliation is no longer a boundary. It used to be if you were a doctor, you were a member of the association of doctors. If you were a Methodist, you went to the Methodist Church. No longer. People feel less bound by tradition to belong, patronize, or be loyal to organizations and businesses that have traditionally served them. If they can be served better by some other organization or business, they will shift their loyalty and participation to the other entity serving their current needs. Just because you are involved in serving a particular audience, that does not mean they have to or will necessarily come to you for their online learning. You will need to establish your credibility and service to them all over again.

Education has to be Financially Self-sufficient

More and more, educational activities such as your online course have to be financially self-sufficient or even make money. Even though you may just be the teacher and not be concerned with the finances of the organization sponsoring your online course, you will want to understand the economics of courses in the Information Age.

Fewer and fewer educational activities can be subsidized or funded. More and more educational activities have to generate sufficient income through registration fees and other means in order to sustain them financially. Here are the financial components of an educational activity:

- Income. This is usually from registration fees, although it could be funded through donations or other sources of income.
- Promotion. This is a cost. Many educational activities require some kind of marketing or promotion to generate participation and enrollments.
- Production. These costs include handouts, materials, and most of all, your fee as a teacher.

New World

Instead of using the boundaries of geography, time, and affiliation, organizations must now position themselves to take advantage of a global niche.

- Administrative. If your course is sponsored by an organization, there will be additional costs to pay for administrative staff and overhead and to support the sponsoring organization.
- Net profit. Some courses may need to generate a net profit for the sponsoring organization.

Promotion is Increasing, Other Costs Declining

In the last century, promotion costs were low, production costs were high, administrative costs were high, and net profits were low for most educational activities. That formula has to change for educational activities to exist successfully in the 21st century. Here's how that will change.

Promotion costs go up. Marketing and promotion costs will continue to grow as a percentage of income. There is simply too much supply, and too many choices for people in their buying. To capture your market, more promotion will be necessary.

Net profits go up. In order to remain competitive and have the funds for future success, organizations, companies and even individuals have to have higher profits. Educational activities are receiving less outside funding. Outside funding will continue to decline. So educational activities, including your online course, will need to make money at some point.

Administrative costs go down. In order for promotion and net profits to go up, something has to go down. Administrative costs need to go down.

Production costs go down. As a percentage of income, production costs have to go down. This impacts you because your pay as a teacher is part of production costs. Your pay does not have to go down as a dollar figure, only as a percentage. That is one reason why we advocate online course enrollments with large numbers, so that more income can be generated and you as a teacher can still receive adequate or good payment for your services.

These relative movements in promotion, production, administration and net profit are valid for most all information service industries, not just educational activities. They are simply the requirements for economic success in the coming century.

Online Economics

Here are some of the economic realities of online learning which will have a growing impact the development and delivery of online courses.

High initial development costs
Face-to-face courses have low fixed costs and high variable costs, while online courses have high fixed costs and low variable costs. What that means is that it is very expensive to develop an online course for a few learners, but there is very little extra cost for additional learners, and very little cost for additional offerings.

Thus, online courses have high initial development costs.

Higher costs coming
Even higher development costs will be coming. When online learners have broadband connections, they will be able to gain access to animation, simulation, video, and interactivity with content.

This will create the demand for even higher quality in online course content. Only those entities with the resources will be able to keep pace with the demand for higher quality.

Shareable content
Once content is created, it can be reused over and over again for little or no cost. It can be much less expensive for a teacher or institution to use content developed by someone else than to try to duplicate the creation of online content.

Original content
Once copyright and intellectual property rights issues are resolved, it is likely that original content will have higher quality than non-original content, and thus be more desirable. High quality original content in the form of shareable content objects (SCOs), or chunks of educational material, are likely to make online course development easier, less expensive and very difficult with which to compete.

Teacher pay must go up
Teacher pay is low using an industrial-age model for online courses, with few students and teachers both developing content and teaching students.

In order for teacher pay to rise and yet remain financially feasible, teachers can either: a) create content and market it widely; or b) purchase or rent content, and devote more time to teaching the students.

A Different Financial Model

Now let's relate these new economic rules to your online course. Many current online courses are operated on the principles of the last century. They have high production, low promotion, and low net profit margins.

A typical online course might have 20 students and charge $500 or so per course. The high price holds down enrollments, and income. There are high production costs, and therefore little left over for net profit.

Price pressure is already driving down online course fees. A recent study by distance learning experts at Regents College in Albany, New York, showed that the average distance learning course fee was $250 and falling. As more people and organizations offer more online courses, the price of an online course will continue to fall.

To gain an advantage, courses will need to have more promotion and marketing. That will be justified if enrollments go up. With larger enrollments, there can be a bigger income for the online course even with lower prices. The new economic environment will call for lower prices, and larger numbers of participants. By being able to teach 100 or more participants online, you will be able to make your online course successful financially.

Chapter 25
Positioning Your
Online Course

In the new environment of the Information Age and the 21st century in which you will be teaching, you will also want to be a marketer of your course. In the old world, you just taught. You didn't worry about getting people to come to your class. Somebody else worried about that. But the marketing of your online course in the new environment is critical. If you do not position your online course properly in the very competitive environment out there, you will not have a long term online success.

There are two absolutely critical aspects of a successful online course that you as teacher have to get right. One is the topic or subject area you will teach. The other critical aspect you have to get right is the target audience.

Choose Your Audience

In positioning a successful online course, the beginning and the end — the alpha and the omega — of success will be the list of names of people you want to attend your program. The list is everything. Show me the names!

Do not expect to be able to post your course with search engines and have people show up. Do not pretend that your course is for everyone. Do not even think that lots of administrators will be begging you to teach for them. And do not think, pretend or expect someone else to do the marketing of your online course for you.

In the new environment, marketing comes first. Teaching comes second. If you have the market, you can deliver the program. If you don't have the market, you don't have anything.

For most online courses, advertising is out of the question, and publicity is hard to get. That leaves the best, most cost-efficient, and most effective way of promoting your course— with direct marketing. Direct marketing involves getting a list of potential participants in your course and then marketing specifically to that list.

So the objective is to define your target audience so clearly and specifically that you can produce the list of names of people in your target audience.

You identify the interest or need that everyone in the list shares. Then show how the interest or need matches your teaching expertise.

Long-term strategy is even more important than short-term success in online course success, because online programming is here to stay. If you can capture the market, you can keep the market. So long term, begin thinking of your audience less in geographic terms and more in terms of interest and need. Think globally.

So if you are a hospital consultant in Maryland, think less of your audience as the hospitals in Maryland, and more in terms of the hospitals in North America. Then think about every hospital in the world. Then think of every hospital in the world with a specific interest or need that matches your expertise. There's your list.

The place to start in defining your online audience is with your current participants, students, members, or customers. This is your core. Build on it. Go after people who look just like your current participants.

You already have a core group of supporters. They already have a positive image of you. You already deliver something of great value to them. This is where to start. This is the foundation upon which you build.

Do not think of going after a totally new audience. Do not think about renting e-mail lists. Do not think about chasing untested and untried lists of names. Develop something very successful for your existing audience. In particular, develop something very successful for your existing audience on the broadest geographical scale possible. Then acquire names of people with the same demographic characteristics as your core present participants.

If you do not choose your target audience, you will not capture your target audience. If you do not capture your target audience, you will lose out to someone else who has more clearly defined her or his audience, and then delivered the kind of online courses that audience wants. As soon as you capture your audience, you can keep your audience. It will be very hard for someone else to take it away from you. So choose your target audience wisely.

Choose the Course Topic

Here are the best measures of success for a topic for an online course:
- Narrow and specific in scope
- Not offered by the competition
- Not offered on-site or in-person
- Compelling, high interest
- Difficult or costly to hear the instructor(s) in-person

Narrow and Specific in Scope

Whatever you offer online should be an offering that you want to be known for, that strengthens your professional image, and will assist you in dominating your knowledge niche.

So the subject areas you want to focus on are those in which you excel, your main bread and butter subject areas with your target audience.

Within the subject areas that match your expertise, narrow the subject area down to a topic that is very narrow and specific in scope. What is "very narrow and specific in scope" will vary according to your target audience. If you are an historian in Australia and teaching a history course to North Americans, the "History of Australia" would be a topic narrow and specific in scope. If you are teaching a history course for Australians, however, the "History of Australia" would NOT be narrow and specific in scope. The "History of Melbourne" might qualify.

Not Offered by the Competition

Welcome to the new world of teaching. It is a world in which you as a teacher have competition. In fact, you have nothing but competition. Everyone out there is an expert. Everyone is a professor. Everyone thinks he knows more about your subject area than you do. It is likely that long term there will be only 1-3 online courses surviving per topic or subject area. The teacher with the most participants will lower the course price to get even more participants, and that teacher will capture the market. So you will need to deal with other online courses and teachers as competition.

You can offer the same courses and programs as is offered by the competition, but it will have a far lesser chance of success than if you offer programs not offered by the competition.

When we talk about "same program" we do not mean the same broad subject area. If your competition offers an online program on computers, that doesn't mean you should avoid offering a computer course online. It

231

does mean you should find a different angle, perspective, sub-specialty or some other distinction that will make your online program different.

Not Offered In-Person or On-Site

One way to enhance your success is to offer topics that your audience cannot get from in-person or on-site seminars or courses. You can have a successful online program competing with an in-person program, but steering clear from in-person program topics will just give you another edge and another opportunity for greater success.

Twenty years from now, all types of subjects and topics will be offered online. But right now, there is a very definite rationale in not competing against a program that is offered in-person or on-site, even or especially if it is offered by your own organization.

The reason is simply that online programs are new and different and our audiences are not used to them. So familiarity and inertia will dictate that many people will opt for the program in-person or on-site.

But if the only way I can get this program is online, then more people will risk the unfamiliarity of online learning because they want so much to learn what you have to offer.

Compelling and High Interest

You can succeed with a program title that is not necessarily compelling or showing high interest with your target audience. But having a compelling and high interest topic will, once again, enhance your chances for success online.

So if there is a "hot" topic with your audience, a current topic area that has just arrived, or a big problem or concern with your audience, find your online program topic there.

One area that has proven successful for many organizations is to offer online programs on such topics as the Internet, World Wide Web, and computers. This kind of program, tailored and specific to your audience segment, is likely to have high interest because the Internet is still so new and everyone eligible for your online program obviously has access to the Internet, so it is a "natural."

Difficulty in Hearing the Presenter/Instructor In-Person

Another way to position your online program for greater success is to promote it to people who cannot hear you in person. And a big bonus to increase online course success is to line up one or more co-presenters or co-instructors not available to your audience for in-person or on-site programs.

The person or persons may not be available for on-site or in-person programs because 1) The travel distance is too great; 2) The person has a busy schedule; or 3) Your audience could not afford what you would have to charge for this person.

For whatever reason, if you can line up an otherwise unavailable presenter or instructor, even for a day, to teach or present online, you will enhance your online program's chances of success.

Not every successful topic has to meet all of the above criteria. Each of the above will give you an additional edge, pull in a few more people, and make it all that much easier for you to score a success with your online programming.

The more advantages your online program has, the more reasons you can give your audience to take your online program, the better your chances of success.

Choosing Your Expertise

At the same time as you are choosing the title, topic or subject area of your online course, you are choosing your area of expertise. Now you may think you already have an area of expertise, you don't need to choose it again.

But in the new world of learning, you will indeed need to choose your area of expertise all over again. Here's why. In the old world of the Industrial Age, which is in decline and will continue to fade, geography was a main determinant of boundaries. That is, you could be the best darn customer service expert in the tri-county area, and that was fine. That nasty big-time customer service author on the coast was so far away he didn't care about invading your tri-county area. But that's all changed. Today that big-time customer service expert can reach your clientele in your tri-county area online.

You no longer have geography as an advantage, or as a defense. To be successful teaching online, you will want to choose an area of expertise in which you can become the foremost authority — even better than that rich author on the coast.

So you will want to become the teacher or presenter as an authority. You should be the best, the foremost authority, the top gun, the best expert, the guru — in whatever you are teaching.

There is no room for the average teacher, the good teacher, the nice guy presenter, the best available presenter in the tri-county area. There is only room in your program for authorities, for the best instructors in the world. Because if you don't have the authority, then someone else does, and then they own your niche. Because why would someone want to take a course from anyone other than the best authority in the world? They don't, they won't.

Some illustrations:
- If Alan Dershowitz, the famous lawyer from Harvard, is hired by an organization to teach his specialty of law, that organization will own its niche. There will be few, if any, attorneys who will want to take the same course from the law professor at Singapore State, as nice as that person is, as great a teacher as that person is. If Alan Dershowitz is a lousy teacher, of course, he loses. But if he is the best, everyone else loses. UNLESS the law professor at Singapore State is an expert in something else — like why Alan Dershowitz is wrong — or has a subspecialty in law — the law of engineering in the state of Wyoming — that Alan Dershowitz doesn't. Then the law professor from Singapore State isn't competing with Alan Dershowitz. She is the world's best expert in another topic, appealing to another niche.
- If you are taking a course on the presidency of Grover Cleveland, you want the best biographer and historian of President Cleveland as your teacher.
- If you are interested in learning about mango trees, you want the foremost authority on mango trees to teach it.

Up until now, instructors could compete offering the same course because of geography (a teacher could not be in New York and Los Angeles at the same time); and because of time (an instructor can teach only so many classes on Tuesday morning). Now those boundaries are gone. The world will need only one to three good courses per topic.

So you will need to be the foremost authority on whatever topic or subject you teach online. Now I will show you how to become the foremost authority in the world.

How to Become the Foremost Authority

In the next few pages, I will show you how to become the world's foremost authority.

While I'm at it, I can also show you how to become the richest person in town. Having lived in Kansas for over 20 years, I spent a lot of time driving through the beautiful Flint Hills of Kansas, with wide open places, few people, and very small towns. It was then it occurred to me how to become the richest person in town. You move to a town which is small enough, and poor enough, that you become the richest person in town. To become the world's foremost authority, you follow the same guidelines.

Here's another illustration. My wife grew up in a town of just 400 people. When she was a little girl, she thought her father was famous. She had proof — everyone in town knew him.

You can turn yourself into the foremost authority in the world. Here's how: Choose a topic area narrow and specific enough that you are the foremost authority in the world.

The two criteria for choosing the topic area: 1) it is narrow or small; and 2) there is no current authority in the topic area.

It is not simply that it is better to be a big fish in a small pond than a small fish in a big pond. In the age of online programming, it is essential that 1) the pond be small; and 2) you are the biggest fish. Otherwise, you get eaten.

Example: You want to do a course on World War II. You are not a famous authority on World War II. Your course stands little chance of success. But you do know more than anyone else, including those famous guys, about the Battle of Strasbourg. Bingo. You are now the foremost authority in the world on the Battle of Strasbourg, now eminently qualified to teach a course on that battle and its implications on the entire war. You have an excellent chance of success with a course on the Battle of Strasbourg.

The above example about our course on World War II rests on one assumption — we want to capture a market of people interested in World War II, and we want to be known as the person with expertise on the Battle of Strasbourg.

With your teaching, the objective is not to start with you and your course and find a market. It is the exact opposite. You start with your market — the target audience — and then you build your course and expertise around the market.

In practice, you already have some kind of target audience, and you have some kind of expertise or niche with that market already. So we are linking needs and resources — your audience's needs with your resources.

We are clarifying our target market — the audience, and our niche — our area of expertise. We are becoming narrower in focus, and more global in visibility.

Chapter 26
A 21st Century Model
for Online Classes

A model for online classes is evolving that provides flexibility and small group student facilitation. The model a) provides students with the content and interaction with the lead teacher, an authority in the field; and b) small group interaction and facilitation.

The most commonly used model for online courses today involves a teacher who develops an online course whose subject matter has traditionally been offered face-to-face. The teacher develops the content and teaches the course to 10-30 students. This industrial age model for online courses is broken and will not remain viable as we move further into the 21st century.

It has these weaknesses:

• Too much teacher time is spent in development.
• An individual teacher or single institution has too few resources for higher quality content delivery.
• Course subjects are duplicated in different institutions, failing to expand the number of subjects offered.
• High development time coupled with teaching time means that reasonable teacher pay is not affordable and thus not available to teachers.
• Tuition costs remain too high for the majority of people in society.
• Discipline experts and authorities are not available to the majority of students.
• Teachers are able to spend less time facilitating and teaching online, and are not able to devote time for professional development in this area.

237

- Not enough learners in society are served to prepare workers for a knowledge economy.
- Too many faculty are engaged in replicating courses instead of creating original courses and knowledge specialities.
- Online courses are either not financially viable for institutions, or they are financially viable only because of low teacher reimbursement.
- Teachers and institutions risk losing academic leadership, uniqueness, faculty and eventually resources, to those teachers and institutions who move to a new model for development and delivery of online courses.

A 21st Century Model for Online Courses

Here's the model:

1. A subject matter teacher who is an authority in a particular subject area develops the content for the online course, using a good deal of material original to the teacher.
2. The course is syndicated. Any college or university that wishes to have one or more of its students participate in the class can purchase a seat in the class for a very low fee.
3. The class, which may number 100 or more students, is divided up into small groups, with an online facilitator or student-centered teacher for each small group.
4. In the large setting, with all students able to participate, the lead instructor provides content, answers questions, creates dialogue, and promotes student discussion.
5. In a small group setting, with 10-32 students, students work with student-centered instructors and each other in more interactive, activity, or project oriented learning, and faculty are able to spend more time with individual students.
6. The fee for the course is low, and the tuition is split between the institution developing and sponsoring the online course and the institution recruiting the student.
7. Credit is awarded by the institution hosting the student, not the institution hosting the course. Each institution sending students to the course may buy-in to a standard set of criteria for the awarding of credit, or may design its own criteria for awarding credit.

The model is not entirely new. It is actually an adaptation of the lecture course model that universities employ, but with a few enhancements for the Internet Age. The syndication concept was first introduced to me by Dorothy Durkin of New York University in 1996.

A number of institutions are already offering online courses with one or more of the characteristics of the model. Some of these institutions in higher education include Athabasca University in Athabasca, Alberta; the University of Nebraska Medical Center in Omaha; the University of North Texas, Denton, Texas; and higher education consultant Aaron Donsky reports a consortium of community colleges in Pennsylvania have developed a similar model.

At the high school level the Virtual High School in Concord, Massachusetts, has developed a similar model. And almost a thousand educational organizations, including colleges, public schools and others, are working with online course providers such as Ed2Go using this model.

Small group facilitation

The small groups can be led by:
- Full professors
- Instructors
- Graduate assistants
- Practitioners and alumni
- Students

The online course greatly expands the possibilities for small-group facilitation. The facilitators no longer have to be local or even at the host institution. Instead, small-group facilitators and learner-oriented teachers can come from other institutions, from other countries around the world, and from the workplace.

The leadership of the small online groups may be what maintains the distinguishing qualities of various institutions of higher education. For example, private colleges might have full professors lead their small groups; universities might have graduate assistants; and community colleges might have their instructors involved with leading the small groups.

The small groups can:
- Meet face-to-face locally;
- Be composed of students from the same institution;
- Be composed of students from different institutions;

Some large online classes might be composed of students from a variety of different institutions. Some participating institutions may choose to have more requirements for course completion than those stipulated by the online course lead instructor.

Here's what happens in the large online class setting:

1. Content is delivered
2. The foremost experts and authorities are teaching
3. Guest lecturers/presenters are possible
4. Discussion takes place
5. Special interest groups can be formed
6. Online tests and quizzes are given

Here's what can happen in the small online group setting:
1. Greater facilitating of discussion
2. Group projects
3. Building a learning community
4. Establishing more cohesive relationships
5. Advising and counseling
6. Grading of individual papers and offline exams
7. Face-to-face meetings
8. Peer-to-peer (student to student) mentoring and sharing

Benefits to Teachers

There are six reasons why teachers with a subject expertise will want to teach online using this model:
1. Pay. Teacher pay will rise substantially. Subject matter teachers will be paid as a percentage of the course income.
2. Authority recognition. With only 1-3 online courses in a given topic area or niche, a teacher will be recognized as an authority.
3. Research. With large numbers of students, comments, and research being undertaken, the teacher can maintain his or her scholarship position and remain a leader in the discipline.
4. Reasonable work. There will be less overwork. Time devoted to the course will be compensated at a reasonable rate.
5. Student resources. Outstanding students can be identified, students become intellectual capital, alumni maintain communication, and the teacher can utilize students as resources.
6. Meets a need. There is an enormous need in society for more knowledge in specialized areas, and an online course teacher fills a gap and meets an information need for society.
7. Consulting. Consulting, writing and speaking all intersect with the teaching of one of the foremost courses in a particular subject area.

Benefits to Facilitators

There are several reasons why teachers who want to spend most or all of their time helping students learn benefit by using this model:

1. Learner-oriented teaching and small-group facilitation become a recognized area of teaching expertise.
2. Teachers will be able to spend more time working with learners, both in small groups and individually.
3. Teachers will be able to devote more work time to teaching, and less work time in administration and non-teaching work.

Online Class Model

I am currently co-teaching a course out of University of North Texas. They have 150 students. There is a lead instructor for the whole class and a co-instructor for each 25 students. The co-instructors handle the discussions, assignments, grading, etc. The lead instructor is responsible for the course content and jumps into the discussions whenever he wants to. Each group of 25 students acts almost like a class by itself. They don't see the other students' posting, only their own group's work. — Dr. Jason Andrew, University of Arkansas, Fayetteville, and the University of North Texas, Denton

---

4. Greater contact time with learners increases the internal rewards for teachers. Teachers will see more visible outcomes and learning behavior changes.

The model that evolves for online classes will probably look like and function as a network. The network has been established as the technical and economic structure for this century, replacing the pyramid. In order for students to work successfully in a network, they need to learn in a network.

While the network model can be used for a small size class, it works well or even better with a larger class size.

Why Larger Class Size is Better: Online

While large class size has been a feature of higher education for the past 100 years, a number of educators have raised questions about the nature of learning in a large online class setting.

Model for Online Courses

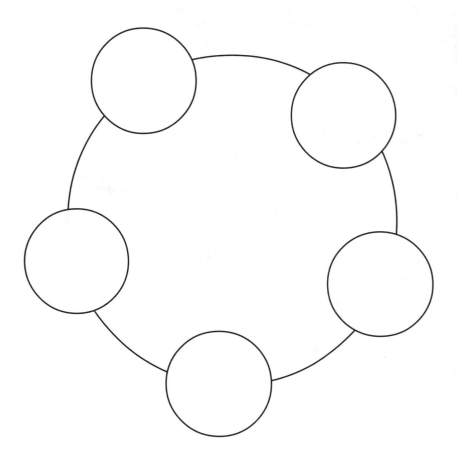

The above model has small discussion groups within a large class.
This provides students with both the "sage on the stage" as well as
the "guide on the side."

Larger class sizes are actually better for online classes than small class sizes.

This author has been interviewed by the *New York Times*, *Los Angeles Times*, and other national media on why the ideal and eventual online course will have an average of 100 or more learners.

There are three reasons why large online classes will become common: 1) It is educationally better for learners; 2) It is demographically inevitable; and 3) It is the only model that is financially and economically feasible.

Educationally Better

The most important reason large online classes will become more prevalent is that more learning occurs in large online classes. Large class size is actually better andragogically (how we learn) than smaller classes.

Here are the top reasons why larger online classes are actually better educationally for the participants.

1. Teacher quality matters most.

Research consistently shows that the quality of the teacher matters more than class size. We can find no research that says that class size is more important than teacher quality.

Teacher education authority Dr. Nancy Zimpher, chancellor of the University of Wisconsin-Milwaukee, recently told the Board of Regents of her state, "The single unequivocal variable that matters most in student success is the quality of the teacher."

Research shows that the quality of the teacher matters more than class size. For example:

"The impact of teacher qualifications was greater than any other single factor (in student success), including class size...." reports the National Commission on Teaching and America's Future..

And Eric Hanushek, an economics professor at the University of Rochester, concluded in a study that the quality of the teacher was more important than class size.

2. Access to the foremost authorities.

With large online classes, learners can have access to, and can afford, the foremost authorities and the best teachers.

With small online classes, access is limited, and too expensive for most people.

3. We learn by interacting.

We learn by interacting: asking questions, responding to others, replying to the instructor. And interaction prompts more interaction. The more interaction, the better. Interaction stimulates ideas, questions, reactions, disagreements. There are more perspectives, points of view, and input.

4. Learners are a resource.

Participants have experiences, perspectives and ideas that are valuable. We used to think of learners as empty vessels, but no longer.

Teachers can tap into this vast wealth of experience and idea sharing to enhance the class and learning for all.

5. Collaborative learning is supported.

Educators are now advocating that participants help each other in the learning process. For example, when one person poses a question, it is far better pedagogy to encourage other students to respond to the question than for the teacher to answer the question immediately.

When other students are engaged in answering questions, they explore more, think more, and share more. It also makes the teacher's input all that more valued.

6. Everyone can talk online.

With in-person or classroom groups, it is possible for only about 35% of the participants to talk during a typical one hour discussion.

But online, everyone can talk. And everyone can talk at the same time. The Internet gives us the opportunity to engage more learners in discussion, a critical learning exercise.

7. Subgroups and specialties can form.

With large online classes, the participants can be divided up into subgroups and specialties if the teacher so chooses.

For example, a class on global politics could have subgroups on European politics, Asian politics, African politics, and so on.
This would not be possible with a small group.

8. Course availability expands.

With syndicated courses, students are able to study many more subject areas. For example, Greek and Roman Religion is offered at only 35 of the nation's 4,000 institutions of higher education. When offered online, all students would be able to study this subject.

Demographically Inevitable

The second major reason why larger online classes will prevail is demographics. Colleges and universities will have no choice. The numbers of instructors will soon decline. The numbers of students will grow substantially.

Walter Stewart of SGI says we already have a "massive shortage of teachers." He estimates by 2010 some two-thirds of faculty will retire, creating what he calls a huge "elder deficit" or knowledge gap.

The only solution is the one higher education resorted to in the sixties and seventies — larger class sizes.

Over the next ten years large numbers of professors in the baby boom generation will retire. The first of the baby boomers reached age 55 in 2001. Only 20% of people over 55 continue to work, according to national statistics. And with the returns of their retirement savings in the stock market over the past decade, a large number of professors are expected to retire by 2010.

At the same time that the pool of higher education instructors declines sharply, the number of college students will grow significantly. First, the baby boomlet generation will reach college age at the same time that the ranks of college teachers declines. Second, the increasing educational demands of the Information Age will create a continuing adult market for higher education.

It will all be too much for institutions to handle. Fortunately the solution— large online classes, is both educationally superior and financially more feasible than small online classes.

Sixties and Seventies

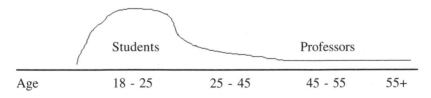

| Age | 18 - 25 | 25 - 45 | 45 - 55 | 55+ |

In the 1960s and 1970s, institutions dealt with the large student population by having large classes of 100-600 students. When this author was in college, there was a dearth of professors and a surplus of students. There was an easy and cost-effective answer: set up more chairs.

For European History, there were 600 enrolled. I would arrive 30 minutes ahead of time to get a seat in the third row of Ag Hall. For Jazz, I sat in the lower balcony of the concert auditorium in the Fine Arts building. For Sociology, we had to find classroom space off campus. But oh, those professors. Harvey Goldberg, the great jazz composer Cecil Taylor, and Hans Gerth, the contemporary and co-author with the legendary sociologist C. Wright Mills. I will never forget them, and what they taught me. I would take those 600-student courses again in a minute.

Eighties and Nineties

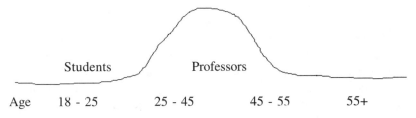

Over the past two decades the baby boomers became teachers and professors, and dealt with the much smaller student population sizes by decreasing class size from 30 to 20 and even 16 students per class.

Next Five to Ten Years

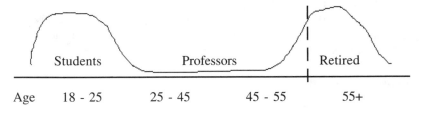

The baby boomers retire. The baby boomlet enters college. The number of teachers and professors is not able to match the increasing student population. Institutions switch back to the earlier model of large class size, only this time the large class size is online.

Financially Feasible

The third major reason why large online classes will prevail is that it is the only model that is financially feasible and economically viable for all concerned: students, teachers, institutions, and society.

Today our educational institutions are in a financial crisis. They are no longer able to educate learners cost effectively. The undesirable results are that education a) is too expensive for most families; and b) consequently education becomes limited, excluding the majority of people.

College costs annually exceed inflation. Graduates from four year colleges can easily acquire $80,000 in debt. Taxpayers are asked to contribute more, and are balking.

Small online classes of 30 or fewer students are also expensive, and uneconomical. In fact, with development costs and instructional costs, they are losing money, costing more than tuition fees.

Of course, universities already offer large F2F classes. At the University of Minnesota, one of the top research and teaching universities in the country, some 30% of lecture classes are larger than 30 students, according to their office of statistics. At Brown University, a parent reported that his son had only one class smaller than 100 students in his first year.

Only large online class sizes can rescue education from its current financially untenable situation. Today most all educators believe only small online classes, those with 10-30 students should be offered. But large online classes, with 100-500 students, offer better and affordable education. Here's why.

1. Large online classes financially allow small face-to-face (F2F) classes. Teachers are freed up to engage learners F2F in smaller class settings.
2. Large online classes are affordable. The costs for a learner plummet from $500 a college course (on average) to less than $100 a course online. This makes higher education affordable for the majority of students in our population.
3. Development costs can be managed. A small online course generates only around $10,000 in income, not enough to cover development costs. With the coming of animation and video, development costs will increase exponentially.
4. Quality teachers can be compensated. Higher education teachers earn an average of $2,500 to teach online courses today, much less than they deserve. It is also much less than what quality teachers require. With a large online class, a professor can earn much more, allowing institutions to retain quality professors.

Higher Education's 21st Century Imperative

With large online classes, higher education can cut tuition in half and double enrollments. Not coincidentally, this is the same challenge (cut costs, increase productivity) facing every 21st century organization, both for-profit and nonprofit.

In 1992, President Clinton noted that a two-year college degree was the entry point into the middle class in America. With the Internet now driving our economy, we know that a four year college degree is required.

Only 29% of our nation's population has a four year college degree, far less than what is needed for a post-industrial society in a knowledge or Information Age economy. In response, last year the Congress authorized over a half million people be able to enter our country to work in high tech and high education jobs because our own population does not currently have the knowledge skills needed.

In 1900, at the dawn of the Industrial Age, fewer than 29% of the population held a high school degree. Society and its schools created universal high school education, even making it a law that a youth attend school through high school. Quite simply, a high school degree was not needed for the Agrarian farm economy of the 19th century. But for the 20th century Industrial Age economy with its factories and offices, a high school degree was essential. Thus by 1998 more than 90% of our population held a high school degree.

At the dawn of the Information or Internet Age, it is clear that workers require a four year college degree to be successful as knowledge workers and maintain a middle class life style. Universal higher education will be provide educated workers for our new economy. To achieve that, large online classes will become key.

Summary

The model described here is gradually becoming adopted in various forms. The development of institutional consortiums and partnerships is one step towards this model.

If you are a teacher, you can be an educational entrepreneur, working independently, with your employing institution, or with other institutions. Innovative teachers are already taking the initiative and creating niche courses in which they are the foremost authority. Create your long term strategy, choose your audience, select your niche topic, develop your online course, then partner with one or more institutions to deliver and market your course.

If you are an administrator, you will want to position your department, school, college or organization for long term success. Choose those relatively few areas in which your organization can be a global leader, where you will have only 2-3 other competitors in your niche market. Work with teachers who are, or can become, the foremost experts, and establish your position.

The opportunities are enormous. There are 100,000 niches, and only a few thousand have been taken. Go for it.

Appendices

Further Reading

From the many excellent sources on teaching online and related subjects, here are the author's favorite recommendations for further reading.

Learning Communities. *Building Learning Communities in Cyberspace*, by Rena Palloff and Keith Pratt, Jossey-Bass Publishers, San Francisco, 1999.

Already a classic, it is the best treatment on the important area of creating an online learning community.

Designing Online Instruction. *The Faculty Guide to Moving Teaching and Learning to the Web*, by Judith Boettcher and Rita-Marie Conrad, League of Innovation, Second edition, 2004.

The best outline on designing online instruction, including such specifics as converting classroom hours to online courses.

Facilitating Online Discussion. *Facilitating Online Learning*, by George Collison, Bonnie Elbaum, Sarah Haavind, and Robert Tinker, Atwood Publishers, Madison, Wisconsin, 2000.

The most in-depth study of facilitating online discussions I have seen, giving this central teaching function with the comprehensive treatment it warrants.

Internet Technology. *How the Internet Works*, by Preston Gralla, Que, Indianapolis, IN, 1999.

After reviewing many other books, I finally found one that is succinct, technical yet understandable, and covers the areas involved in the technology of online learning.

Internet Age. *Net Gain*, by John Hagel III and Arthur G. Armstrong, Harvard Business School Press, 1996.

My first "ah ha" book explaining the Internet Age and virtual community and life in the 21st century. Essential for understanding where society is going.

Personal Transition. *The Great Crossover: Personal Confidence in the Age of the Microchip*, by Dan Sullivan, The Strategic Coach, Toronto, 1997.

A wonderfully helpful book to help in the personal transition from the Industrial Age to the Internet Age, explained on a personal level, with how-to practical tips.

How We Learn. *The Adult Learner: A Neglected Species*, by Malcolm Knowles, Gulf Publishing, Houston, 1998.

This classic on andragogy, the study of how we learn, is the fundamental basis upon which teaching in the 21st century must be based.

Learning Online. *Learning OntheNet*, by William A. Draves, LERN, River Falls, WI, 2001.

For online learners and potential online learners, original research and practical how-to tips for learning online.

Growing Up Digital. *Growing Up Digital: The Rise of the Net Generation*, by Don Tapscott, McGraw-Hill, New York, NY, 1998.

The best treatment on young people and the Internet, and what they have to teach us.

FAQs

Here are some of the more frequently asked questions (FAQs) teachers ask about teaching online, followed by the chapter in which the question is addressed:

Q1. How much time does it take to develop an online course? (Chapter 10)

Q2. How much do teachers get paid for teaching online? (Chapter 10)

Q3. Who owns the online course? (Chapter 7)

Q4. How often should I go online during the course? (Chapter 15)

Q5. How often should students log on every week? (Chapter 15)

Q6. How do I prevent cheating online? (Chapter 13)

Q7. How much does it cost to develop an online course? (Chapter 10)

Q8. What are the best testing or exam methods for online courses? (Chapter 13)

Q9. Should I use video? (Chapter 10)

Q10. Should I use a live chat? (Chapter 12)

Q11. How can I keep up with all the e-mails coming from students? (Chapter 12)

Q12. How long should modules or units last? (Chapter 9)

Q13. How much on-screen copy should be in a "chunk"? (Chapter 10)

Q14. How long should audio presentations be? (Chapter 11)

Q15. How much of the course will I have to revise each time? (Chapter 16)

Q16. How many comments should each student make each week? (Chapter 12)

Advanced Quiz

If you think you might know just about everything in this book, take this quiz. This is not a trivia test; each quiz question is based on an advanced concept important to teaching online.

If you get half or more of the questions correct, please contact me, as you have much valuable expertise to share. If you get fewer than half of the questions correct, then I think you'll find this book has some advanced material as well as unique information not available anywhere else.

1. Who invented the World Wide Web?
2. What does the emoticon ^5 mean?
3. What is metadata?
4. P2P stands for?
5. What is a shared content object, or SCO?
6. What is Moore's Law?
7. True or false: Every online course is now a published work?
8. High fixed costs, low variable costs, is true for F2F or online courses?
9. The hardest place to learn online is in the bedroom, kitchen, home office or office at work?
10. What is peak learning time?
11. What is a WebQuest?
12. Who owns an online course?
13. Can you teach critical thinking online?
14. What is retinal identification?
15. What is andragogy?
16. What percent of participants make comments in a good F2F discussion?
17. Do learning styles differ by generation?

Basic Course Readiness Guidelines

The following are basic course readiness guidelines almost all online courses should follow.

1. Do students receive e-mail and mail confirmations after registering with orientation information about taking a course online?
2. Do students take an online orientation to online learning?
3. Is there technical support help service for your students?
4. Is there a plan for getting in touch with students if the server goes down?
5. Do you have a phone number to contact your techie on a 24-hour basis?
6. Do you have a technical person or team for your course?
7. Have you and your technical support staff met to discuss monitoring your course?
8. Is there a textbook or set of readings for your course?
9. Is the course divided into 5-15 modules or units?
10. Is the online copy chunked?
11. Is the online copy supplemental to the readings (answer 'yes') or the primary source of readings (answer 'no') for the course?
12. Do you have a written agreement with your institution about who owns the course and content?
13. Are you trained and comfortable with all the functions of your online classroom software?
14. Have you secured copyright permission for any non-original material (not covered by the Fair Use Guidelines) used in the course?
15. Do you have any instructional media, such as pictures, audio, simulations and so on, other than the online copy for your course?
16. Have you dealt with web accessibility issues for any students with visual or hearing disabilities?
17. Do you have discussion questions and starter comments for online discussion for each of your units?
18. Do you have guidelines and rules for online discussion for your students?
19. Do your students understand the online discussion guidelines and rules?
20. Do you have unit quizzes?
21. Do you have a final exam, group project, individual project, or

other course evaluation activities determined?
22. Do you have grading criteria determined for your course?
23. Do students understand the grading criteria for your course?
24. Are online discussion comments a part of the student's grade?
25. Will all discussion related to the course and course content be conducted in the threaded discussion area?
26. Will you be logging into your online course at least once a day (not necessarily on weekends) during the course?
27. Have you set aside the time and created a way to "break the ice" and help students get acquainted online the first week of the course?
28. Do you have a welcome page with instructions and notes for each unit?
29. Do you have a policy to limit e-mail to personal and individual student issues?
30. Do you have one or more physical settings where you can teach online without distraction and interruption?
31. Do you have a method of gaining student feedback about your course?

Best Practices Checklist

The following are many, if not most, of the practices that the best online teachers engage in their online courses. These practices have been garnered from comments from experienced online teachers, recommendations from online learning experts, and workshops presented at national conferences on online learning.

Few, if any, online courses display all of the following attributes and practices. Not all may be relevant to the subject matter you are teaching. Instead, they represent "targets" for online teachers who want to enhance the quality of their online courses by following the most commonly used and accepted best practices.

Just for fun, check those which you currently do to see how advanced your online course may be. Make a note to yourself with 1-3 other best practices you feel are as important as the ones listed here.

1. Do you have your class divided into smaller discussion groups?
2. Do you provide additional points for online discussion comments that are responses and replies to other comments?
3. Do you encourage or mandate that students help each other, answer each other's questions online, or otherwise assist and engage in sharing in the group?
4. Do you do role plays, online debates, group presentations, or other stimulating variations for student interaction online?
5. Have you turned some of your quizzes into games?
6. Do you have audio lectures online?
7. Do you have synchronized slides with your audio lectures online?
8. Do you have multiple ways of evaluation and grading?
9. Do you have unit self-quizzes with which the student can gain feedback, but are not a part of the student's grade?
10. Do you have a separate discussion area for non-course related chat for your students?
11. Do you have group projects or any collaborative team activities?
12. Do you utilize WebQuests, virtual tours, or other online resource activities?
13. Do you utilize any guest presenters or outside content experts?
14. Do you have any instructional help in facilitating the small discussion groups?
15. Do you have any content in which the student can interact?
16. Do you have any simulations?

17. Do you have any interactive simulations?
18. Do you save student testimonials about your course to share with future students?
19. Do you select 1-5 things to improve before your next offering?

Why half of learning will be online in the 21st century

The forecast, while based on current data and projected trends, is also meant to convey that learning in this century will be a balance of face-to-face (F2F) and online. The author would accept any estimates between 30% and 70% as supportive of that balance. The percentage is likely to differ by audience and type of education as well. For example, elementary school is likely to be more F2F than online learning, while workforce training is projected to be more than half online.

1. According to the American Society for Training and Development (ASTD), some 35% of workforce training is now mediated. This is already close to half.

2. Historically, higher education has prepared students for the workforce. And historically, business needs have helped influence education. For example, in the 1920s business and education leaders incorporated "Industrial Education" into the high school curriculum (See Child Labor, by Julia E. Johnsen, 1925).

Today, business leaders are calling upon higher education to incorporate "Technical Education" into the curriculum (see for example, *Minneapolis Star Tribune*, March 5, 2001).

3. If workers are learning online in their work, employers will recruit students who have the skills and abilities to learn online. The first university to REQUIRE students to take online courses is Farleigh Dickinson University (*Chronicle of Higher Education*, September 2000) . The first public school district to REQUIRE students to take online courses is Toronto Public Schools (source: conversation with Ken Harvey, Principal, Distance Education School, Greater Vancouver Public Schools, Vancouver, BC, January 2001).

4. As the forecast notes, there will be a mix. The percentage is likely to be different for elementary, secondary, undergraduate, graduate, workplace, and continuing education. Taken all together, over a life span, the percentage is likely to be around half by 2050.

5. The Vice President of Human Resources for Sprint forecast at a 1996 education conference (Kansas City, October 1996, American Association of Adult and Continuing Education) that 90% of learning would be online.

However, the work of Dr. Jerold Apps (*Mastering the Teaching of Adults, The Heartful Teacher*) and Dr. Steven Brookfield (*Discussion as a Way of Teaching*) clearly point out the areas in which F2F learning and teaching are an important part of life.

6. On the other hand, educators who forecast that online learning will have a minimal impact on education are also likely not to be supported by the continued growth of online learning.

In 2001, over a million students were engaged in online learning (US Distance Education Association) and about 75% of colleges and universities were offering online courses (*Chronicle of Higher Education*).

This is clearly a strong initial move into online learning. With online learning only five years old, the rate of adoption is significantly higher than that for educational television (for example) five years after the initiation of television. In fact, neither educational television nor distance learning ever reached the registrations and interest currently shown with online learning.

7. Walter Stewart of SGI, in a keynote address at the World Education Market conference in Vancouver, BC, in May 2001, noted that continuing education and training expenditures continue to rise, indicating that learning will continue to be incorporated into work. Credit Suisse projects that by 2005 continuing education expenditures will reach $40 billion, while U.S. corporations will spend an additional $58 billion on training.

Learning will become an integral if hardly perceptible part of the average employee's workday. "Do we even know or care when we are learning or producing today? He noted. "If you can't tell the difference, why be in a different place to do it?"

References

Chapter 1

The Wizard of Oz and L. Frank Baum information from a talk by history professor Dr. Robert Luehrs, Fort Hays State University, Hays, Kansas, funded by the Kansas Humanities Council.
Other references to Kansas history in the late nineteenth century are from exhibits at the Kansas Historical Museum, Topeka, Kansas.
The reference to Kansas having mandatory continuing education on the The Wizard of Oz is poetic license, and not true.

Chapter 2

The Gerald Celente quote is from his book, *Trends 2000*, Warner Books, New York, NY, 1997, page 249.
From *The Virtual Classroom: Learning without limits via computer networks*, by Starr Roxanne Hiltz, 1994, Ablex Publishing, Norwood, NJ.
Washington Post references from *Teaching Online*, by Debbie Goldberg, *Washington Post* web site, April 5, 1998.
For background information on the plow and tractor, I am indebted to Professor Andrew Barkley, Department of Agricultural Economics, Kansas State University, Manhattan, Kansas.
Reference to the military and cavalry from *FDR: Into the Storm*, by Kenneth S. Davis, 1993.
Reference to one-room school houses in the State of Washington from *Encyclopedia Britannica*, Volume 23, page 389, University of Chicago, Chicago, Illinois, 1945.
Peter J. Denning's quote is from his manuscript, "How We Will Learn," October 1996, George Mason University, Fairfax, Virginia, page 2.
Reference to Keio University from "Japan Shuts Down Its Education Assembly Line," by Gale Eisenstodt, *Fast Company* magazine, February/March 1997, pages 40-42.
For more on self-directed learning and adult education, see Malcolm Knowles *The Adult Learner: A Neglected Species*, 1973, Gulf Publishing, Houston, page 42.
Several Internet references are owed to Richard Thieme, consultant and futurist, Fox Point, Wisconsin, from a speech at the Metcom conference, April 4, 1996, Chicago.
University Online Publishing reference to online courses from Dees Stallings, University Online Publishing, Fairfax, Virginia.

Distance and online learning data from Paula Peinovich, Regents College, Albany, NY.

For the seminal and best work on virtual community, see *Net Gain* by John Hagel and Arthur G. Armstrong, Harvard Business School Press, Boston, 1997. Another excellent related work is *Cybercorp*, by James Martin, Amacom Books, New York, NY, 1996.

Positioning is a classic marketing book by Al Ries and Jack Trout, 1981, first edition.

Chapter 3

The best book on integrative learning and in-person teaching is *Mastering the Teaching of Adults* by Jerold Apps, Krieger Publishing, Melbourne, Florida, 1991.

The term "web enhanced" courses is from *The Faculty Guide for Moving Teaching and Learning to the Web*, by Judith Boettcher and Rita-Marie Conrad, League of Innovation, 1999.

Chapter 4

For more on the history of the Internet, see "The Portable Learn the Net" by Michael Lerner, available at www.learnthenet.com.

For more on Tim Berners-Lee and his invention of the World Wide Web, see *Weaving the Web* by Tim Berners-Lee, Harper San Francisco, San Francisco, 1999.

The hard copy back-up recommendation is from *The Online Teaching Guide*, Ken H. White and Bob H. Weight, page 81.

The Amy Finch quote is from LERN's online course, "Building Learning Communities in Cyberspace," with Rena Palloff and Keith Pratt, July 2001.

Chapter 5

For more on what an online classroom looks like, see the web sites of three popular online classroom providers at www.Blackboard.com, www.WebCT.com, and www.eCollege.com.

Chapter 6

Comments from the father of a bright teenager from an interview by Margo Adler on National Public Radio, April 28, 2000.

The "glob" quote is from "Customizing the Learning Experience with Reusable Content Objects," by Susan Kirshbaum, speech, LearningByte International seminar, April 23, 2000, St. Paul, Minnesota.

Guenther Weydauer's comments are from his keynote address, LERN's Learning Online 2001 conference, June 25, 2001, Minneapolis. "All teaching becomes publishing" is from a Copyright and Intellectual Property panel discussion, World Education Market conference, Vancouver, Canada, May 24-26, 2001.

Chapter 7

Panel discussion on copyright and intellectual property issues was at World Education Market, May 2001, Vancouver, BC, Canada. Panelists included James Mitchell, UK; Piero Attanasio, Italy; Terence Dixon, USA; Steve Epstein, USA; and Richard McCracken, UK.

Palloff & Pratt name copyright and intellectual property issues as a top concern in their book, *Lessons from the Cyberspace Classroom*, Jossey-Bass Publishers, San Francisco, 2001, page xiv.

Ko and Rossen's notes on fair use guidelines are from their book, *Teaching Online*, by Susan Ko and Steve Rossen, Houghton Mifflin Company, Boston, page 181.

Fair Use Guidelines for Educational Multimedia, adopted by the Subcommittee on Courts and Intellectual Property, Committee on the Judiciary, U.S. House of Representatives, September 27, 1996, from http://www.unt.edu/cdl/services/fairuse.htm.

Craig R. Barrett was interviewed by the *New York Times*, July 29, 2001.

Walter Stewart's comments are from his speech at the World Education Market, May 2001, Vancouver, BC.

Stephen Downes's comments were from an interview with this author May 26, 2001.

Chapter 9

Dr. Rita-Marie Conrad's comment about keeping a three-credit online course at 16 weeks in length was made while teaching LERN's "Teaching Online" online course February 5, 2001.

Conrad's estimate of 135 hours of student work is from the book, *The Faculty Guide for Moving Teaching and Learning to the Web*, by Judith Boettcher and Rita-Marie Conrad, League of Innovation, 1999.

Moving a course from the traditional classroom to online from Boettcher and Conrad, page 54.

Managing student files from Ko and Rossen, page 212.

Chapter 10

"Digital correspondence courses are in decline," and "There is no such thing as a canned course," Dr. Rita-Marie Conrad, Keynote, Learning Online 2001, June 26, 2001, Minneapolis.

Ed Stephan's web site is http://www.ac.wwu.edu/~stephan/Animation/ animation.html

Peter Cochrane's simulation was demonstrated at the 15th Annual Distance Teaching and Learning Conference, Madison, Wisconsin, August 1999.

Dr. Dan Lim, "Designing Online Animated Tutorials," 17th Annual Distance Teaching and Learning Conference, Madison, Wisconsin, August 2001.

Development time estimate is from Boettcher and Conrad, page 81.

Web accessibility guidelines from Alice Anderson and Brian Bundy session, "Web Accessibility," at the 17th Annual Distance Teaching and Learning Conference, Madison, Wisconsin, August 2001.

Dr. Rod Riegle, Illinois State University, demonstrating his online gaming course in education at Distance Teaching and Learning Conferences, Madison, Wisconsin, 1999 and 2004.

Chapter 11

Eudora Welty comment from the *New York Times*, July 26, 2001, quoting a 1984 book by Welty.

Information on synchronizing PowerPoint, slides and storyboards from Les Howles, University of Wisconsin- Madison, in a LERN online course "Creating Streaming Audio on the Web" taught by Howles in July 2001.

Chapter 12

Palloff and Pratt quote, from *Building Learning Communities in Cyberspace*, Jossey-Bass Publishers, San Francisco, 1999, page 15, and page 5.

Collison, George; Elbaum, Bonnie; Haavind, Sarah, and Tinker, Robert, *Facilitating Online Learning*, Atwood Publishing, Madison, Wisconsin, 2000, page 2.

Conrad quote, from LERN's "Teaching Online" course, October 2000.

Collison et al, pages 142-143.

Debbie Weil, Washington, DC, "The Next Big Online Thing," keynote at LERN Annual Conference, Las Vegas, 2005.

Chapter 13

William Horton, William Horton Consulting, "It's not the technology, stupid!" keynote at 17th Annual Conference on Distance Teaching and Learning, Madison, Wisconsin, August 2001. For more, see his web site at www.horton.com.

Boys and Girls Learn Differently! By Michael Gurian, Jossey-Bass, San Francisco, 2001.

Gender and Fair Assessment, by Warren Willingham and Nancy S. Cole, Educational Testing Service, 1997.

"Smart Boys Bad Grades," by Julie Coates and William A. Draves, Learning Resources Network, 2006.

Engaging the Online Learner, Rita-Marie Conrad and J. Ana Donaldson, Jossey-Bass, San Francisco, 2004.

Diana Laurillard, U.K. Department of Education and Training, London, presentation at Sussex Headmasters Conference, March 2006.

Nine Shift: Work, life and education in the 21ˢᵗ century, William A. Draves and Julie Coates, Learning Resources Network, 2004.

Chapter 14

Conrad, June 2001 speech.

Palloff and Pratt, page 21.

Boettcher and Conrad, pages 91-92.

Palloff and Pratt, page 76.

Jerry Apps, from *Mastering the Teaching of Adults*, by Jerold Apps, 1991, Krieger Publishing, Melbourne, Florida.

Russell Robinson's work is from *Helping Adults Learn and Change*, Omnibook Company, Milwaukee, Wisconsin, 1979, page 50.

Philip C. Candy's work is from *Self-Direction for Lifelong Learning*, Jossey-Bass Publishers, San Francisco, CA, 1991, page 391.

Florence Nelson's work is from *Yes, You Can Teach*, Carma Press, St. Paul, MN, 1977, page 4.

"Revitalizing Your Course Mid-way," online presentation and article by Roberta Ross-Fisher of St. Louis, Walden University, *LERN Magazine*, September 2001.

"Continuous Engagement," by Dr. Mary Dereshiwsky, Northern Arizona University, *LERN Magazine*, October 2005.

Chapter 15

Collison, et al, page 49.

Palloff and Pratt, page 103.

Conrad and Crowell citation from Palloff and Pratt, page 51.
Emoticon definition from Collison, et al.
Key facilitator roles from Collison, et al, pages 106, 108, 110, 112, 115, 118, and 125.
Volley of views, Palloff and Pratt, page 119.
Frustration, Palloff and Pratt, page 103.
Get into your course once a day, Palloff and Pratt, page 107.

Chapter 16

Dr. Mary Moretto, "Quality Assurance and Course Readiness" session, Learning Online 2001, LERN, June 2001, Minneapolis.

Chapter 17

For the best book on how adults learn, see *The Adult Learner: A Neglected Species*, by Malcolm Knowles. Originally published in 1973, it is frequently updated and is a classic in the field of adult education

Documentation on our knowledge society comes from Peter Cochrane, lead researcher from British Telecom, in a speech at the 16th Annual Distance Learning and Teaching Conference at the University of Wisconsin in 1999.

Knowledge society organizations. For more on how organizations are being restructured for the Information Age, see "The Coming of the New Organization," by Peter Drucker, *Harvard Business Review*, January-February 1998.

Are you right for online learning? You could see "What Makes a Successful Online Learner," at http://illinois.online.uillinois.edu/model/Studentprofile.htm, (at the time of printing, URLs often change), which also had links to other web sites on online learning for students.

Where you will work and learn. See for example, the business management guru Peter Drucker's article in *Fortune*, May 1997, in which he predicts and advocates the tearing down of university buildings, buildings being irrelevant or even detrimental in the 21st century.

How we will learn. For more reasons and the rationale behind online learning, see "How We Will Learn" by Peter J. Denning, George Mason University, published in *Beyond Calculation*, Copernicus, March 1997.

Learning in the future. For more on the transformation of learning and education in the 21st century, see "Learning will become interactive," an interview with Peter Hutchison, *Minneapolis Star Tribune*, October 27, 1998.

Chapter 18

Projected learning online. Several sources contributed to this projection, such as the estimated market for training delivered via technology in "Taking the E-train," Christa Degnan, *PC Week Online*, May 31, 1999.

Adults and technology. The best, most kind treatment of adults' ability to conquer technology in relationship to younger people is the chapter The Generation Lap in *Growing Up Digital: The Rise of the Net Generation,* by Don Tapscott, McGraw-Hill, 1998, and at www.growingupdigital.com

Chapter 19

How young people learn online. See the chapter N-Gen Learning in *Growing Up Digital: The Rise of the Net Generation*, the best treatment on young people and the Internet, by Don Tapscott, McGraw-Hill, 1998, and at www.growingupdigital.com

How young people learn online. See also the work of Jaron Lanier, lead scientist for the Tele-Immersion Institute, and keynote speaker at Online Learning 2000, Denver, Colorado.

"Online courses will be of higher quality than the traditional classroom and provide more individual attention," William A. Draves, *New York Times*, September 5, 1997.

Quality of distance learning. For more on the quality of distance learning, see the article "Teaching Online" by Debbie Goldberg, *Washington Post*, April 5, 1998.

Genuine learning. For more on how we learn online, see *Hyperlearning, the New Technology and the End of Education*, by Lewis J. Perelman, 2000.

Generational Learning Styles, by Julie Coates, Learning Resources Network, 2007.

Chapter 20

Introduction to online learning. The author researched various web sites and online classrooms. For example, see "An Introduction to On-Line Instruction" by Dees Stallings, Vcampus, Fairfax, Virginia.

Virtual community. For the best explanation of virtual community, see *Net Gain* by John Hagel III and Arthur G. Armstrong, Harvard

Business School Press.

Online culture. For how people behave and interact online, see *Cyberville* by Stacy Horn, Warner Books.

Chapter 21

Chip prices. The information about chip prices in 2010, plus the growth of information chart, and information on Moore's Law were gained from a speech by Peter Cochrane, the lead researcher for British Telecom, at the 15th Annual Distance Learning and Teaching Conference in Madison, Wisconsin. Cochrane writes a column for the *London Daily Telegraph*. You can find out more about him and his writing at www.bp.com/cochrane.

The Future. For more interesting and well founded thoughts on life in the 21st century, see *Trends 2000*, by Gerald Celente, Warner Books, 1997.

Your pyramid is collapsing. For the best work on how organizational structures will change to adapt to the 21st century, see *The Great Crossover: Personal Confidence in the Age of the Microchip* by Dan Sullivan, The Strategic Coach, Toronto, 1997.

Chapter 22

"History of Frankfort, Kansas," from the Frankfort, Kansas, Library, June Warren, librarian.

Chapter 24

The One to One Future, by Don Peppers and Martha Rogers, Doubleday, New York, NY, 1993.

Chapter 26

Telephone interview with Dorothy Durkin, November 1996. When told of another institution's varied online offerings, Durkin responded "That's too much inventory," thus introducing me to the idea of establishing leadership in a few niche areas, and the concept of syndication.

Regarding the Pennsylvania Virtual Community College Consortium, see "An Online Delivery Model Starts to Emerge" by Aaron Donsky, *LERN Magazine*, July-August, 2001.

Chapter 27

Dr. Nancy Zimpher's comments made in testimony before the Board of Regents, State of Wisconsin, May 24, 2001, meeting in River Falls, Wisconsin.

The impact of teacher qualifications report by the National Commission on Teaching and America's Future was reported in a story "Better teachers is reform movement" by Alan J. Borsuk, *The Milwaukee Journal*, February 2000.

Eric Hanushek's study was reported in "Studies on Class Size," by Michael Pollak, *New York Times*, February 1999.

Number of colleges offering Greek and Roman Religion, according to a listing of college courses by Market Data Retrieval.

Walter Stewart's comments were made at World Education Market, May 2001, Vancouver, BC.

College debt, as heard on "Sound Money," Minnesota Public Radio, June 2000.

For arguments on 'scalability' in adhering to small class sizes of 10-30, see, for example, Charles Karelis, executive director of the Fund for the Improvement of Postsecondary Education (FIPSE), as quoted in *Higher Education in an Era of Digital Competition*, by Donald Hanna and Associates, pages 109-112. Hanna appears to support Karelis's position, as do many other educators.

Current online course costs from a survey of online college course costs at lifelonglearning.com.

Lower online course fees from a survey of large class size online course offerings.

Four-year degree completion statistics from *World Fact Book*, 1999 edition.

Average online course teacher pay from survey at 16th Annual Distance Learning and Teaching conference, Madison, August 2000.

Higher online teacher salaries have been documented, in one case reported to this writer by a university official who asked to remain anonymous.

Lack of knowledge skills needed, from the *New York Times*, November 2000.

1900 statistics on high school completion from *Statistical History of the United States*.

Bibliography

Berners-Lee, T., *Weaving the Web*, Harper San Francisco, San Francisco, 1999.

Boettcher, J. and Conrad, R., *Faculty Guide for Moving Teaching and Learning to the Web*, League for Innovation in the Community College, 1999.

Bridges, W., *Managing Transitions*, Perseus Books, Reading, MA, 1991.

Cochrane, P., "Can We All Be Polymaths?" Annual Distance Learning and Teaching Conference, Madison, WI, August 1999.

Collison, G., Elbaum, B., Haavind, S. and Tinker, R., *Facilitating Online Learning: Effective Strategies for Moderators*, Atwood Publishing, Madison, WI, 2000.

Conrad, R., "What We Know, What We Don't Know," LERN Annual Conference, Minneapolis, MN, June 2001.

Cotton, E., *The Online Classroom*, ERIC Clearinghouse, Bloomington, IN, 1998.

Cuban, L., *Teachers and Machines: The Classroom Use of Technology Since 1920*, Teachers College Press, New York, 1986.

Draves, W., *How to Teach Adults, Second Edition*, LERN, River Falls, WI, 1998.

Draves, W., *Learning OntheNet*, LERN, River Falls, WI, 2001.

Draves, W., *Energizing the Learning Environment*, LERN, River Falls, WI, 1994.

Ellis, D., *Becoming a Master Student*, Houghton Mifflin Company, Boston, 2000.

Gilbert, S., *How to Be a Successful Online Student*, McGraw-Hill, New York, 2001.

Gralla, P., *How the Internet Works*, Que, Indianapolis, IN, 1999.

Hall, B., *Web-Based Training Cookbook*, John Wiley & Sons, Inc., New York, 1997.

Hanna, D., *Higher Education in an Era of Digital Competition*, Atwood Publishing, Madison, WI, 2000.

Hanna, D., Glowacki-Dudka, M., and Conceicao-Runlee, S., *147 Practical Tips for Teaching Online Groups*, Atwood Publishing, Madison, WI, 2000.

Ko, S. and Rossen, S., *Teaching Online*, Houghton Mifflin Company, Boston, 2001.

Palloff, R. and Pratt, K., *Building Learning Communities in Cyberspace*, Jossey-Bass Publishers, San Francisco, 1999.

Palloff, R. and Pratt, K., *Lessons from the Cyberspace Classroom*, Jossey-Bass Publishers, San Francisco, 2001.

Palloff, R. and Pratt, K., "Lessons from the Cyberspace Classroom," LERN Annual Conference, Minneapolis, MN, May 2001.

Stewart, W., "The Knowledge Economy," World Education Market, Vancouver, BC, May 2001.

Tapscott, D., *Growing Up Digital*, McGraw-Hill, New York, 1998.

"Teaching Online," online course; April 2000, May 2000, October 2000, February 2001, April 2001, May 2001, LERN.

White, K. and Weight, B., *The Online Teaching Guide*, Allyn and Bacon, Needham Heights, MA, 2000.

Certified Online Instructor — Featuring the foremost authorities:

"Building Learning Communities in Cyberspace"
Dr. Rena Palloff and Dr. Keith Pratt, authors of the best-selling book of the same title

"Designing Online Instruction"
Dr. Rita-Marie Conrad, author of *The Faculty Guide for Moving Teaching and Learning to the Web*

"Teaching Online"
William A. Draves, author of *Teaching Online* and *Learning OntheNet,* and Dr. Rita-Marie Conrad

About LERN

The Learning Resources Network (LERN) is the leading association in lifelong learning programming, offering information and consulting expertise to providers of lifelong learning programs.

Begun in 1974, LERN serves more than 9,000 professionals every year by providing practical, how-to information on marketing, finances, management, and product development. It is information not available anywhere else.

Services include publications; newsletters; seminars, conferences, Institutes and in-house training programs; and consulting to members and others. LERN's Internet Information Services include more than 450 reports on the management and marketing of continuing education programming; online discussions with colleagues from around the world; news; surveys, and more.

LERN serves a wide variety of institutions, including state universities, four-year colleges, colleges within universities, private colleges, community colleges, technical colleges, public schools, recreation departments, and associations.

Every year we research and disseminate the most advanced and sophisticated information. Recent work has included: profit margins—what makes money; redesigning of job descriptions; the information specialist position; an action strategy for internal marketing; developing a product mix for your segments; why you need seven market segments; the shift from products to markets; and how to measure staff time.

LERN is a nonprofit, tax-exempt, educational organization. We are led by a Board of Directors, with daily operations carried out by 20 staff and consultants located in three offices around the country.

LERN's mission is to extend lifelong learning to all. Our vision statement is: "to be the authoritative, distinctive source of practical information related to lifelong learning programs." Our slogan is *"Information That Works!"*®

Bulk Discounts

Order for everyone in your organization!

Up to 50% off!

25+ copies, just $9.95 each (50% off)!
For 100+ copies, contact LERN at *info@lern.org* or 800-678-5376.

_____
Name

_____
Title or Department (if any)

_____
Organization

_____
Address

_____
City, State/Province, ZIP/Postal Code

_____
E-mail Address   Phone

Please send _____(#) **copies**
of *Advanced Teaching Online,*
3rd ed., **by William A. Draves**
at _____ **(price per copy).**

Subtotal $_____

Shipping $_____

Total $_____

Please check one:

____Payment enclosed.

____Charge my credit card.

Shipping and Handling:
Please call 800-678-5376 or
send e-mail to *info@lern.org*
for current shipping information.

_____
Account #   Exp.

_____
Cardholder's Name (please print)

_____
Cardholder's Signature

To Order *Advanced Teaching Online*

Call: 800-678-5376 (US and Canada)
Fax, toll-free: 888-234-8633 (worldwide)
E-mail: info@lern.org
Web: http://www.lern.org
Mail to: LERN Books, PO Box 9, River Falls, WI 54022 USA